"The doctrine of Sc⸻, and Nichols and Brandt have provided us with a comprehensive survey of approaches to the doctrine of Scripture, showing the drift among evangelical and Reformed theologians over the past century from a commitment to Scripture's infallibility/inerrancy. This book deserves careful reading even by those who are familiar with the plot-lines of the issue. It would be difficult to exaggerate the timeliness of this book."

—DEREK W. H. THOMAS, John E. Richards Professor of Theology, Reformed Theological Seminary; Minister of Teaching, First Presbyterian Church, Jackson, Mississippi

"*Ancient Word, Changing Worlds* is the best, clearest, and most reliable historical overview of the doctrine of Scripture for a contemporary audience. As careful historians, Nichols and Brandt show what the church has always believed about the Bible as the Word of God, and also how our understanding of the inspiration, inerrancy, and interpretation of Scripture has grown through the centuries. The authors let scholars and theologians on all sides of the age-old battle for the Bible speak in their own words, giving us the historical context and theological framework we need to accept the Bible's own witness to its beauty, perfection, and divine authority."

—PHILIP RYKEN, Senior Minister, Tenth Presbyterian Church, Philadelphia

ANCIENT WORD, CHANGING WORLDS

Other books by Stephen J. Nichols:

Jonathan Edwards:
A Guided Tour of His Life and Thought. (2001)

Martin Luther:
A Guided Tour of His Life and Thought. (2002)

An Absolute Sort of Certainty:
The Holy Spirit and the Apologetics of Jonathan Edwards. (2003)

The Legacy of Jonathan Edwards:
American Religion and the Evangelical Tradition (co-editor). (2003)

J. Gresham Machen:
A Guided Tour of His Life and Thought. (2004)

Heaven on Earth:
Capturing Jonathan Edwards's Vision of Living in Between.
Crossway Books, (2006)

Pages from Church History:
A Guided Tour of Christian Classics. (2006)

The Reformation:
How a Monk and a Mallet Changed the World. Crossway Books, (2007)

For Us and for Our Salvation:
The Doctrine of Christ in the Early Church. Crossway Books, (2007)

Jesus Made in America:
A Cultural History from the Puritans to The Passion of the Christ. (2008)

Getting the Blues:
What Blues Music Teaches Us about Suffering and Salvation. (2008)

ANCIENT WORD, CHANGING WORLDS

the Doctrine *of* Scripture *in a* Modern Age

STEPHEN J. NICHOLS & ERIC T. BRANDT

CROSSWAY

WHEATON, ILLINOIS

Cover design: Jon McGrath

Cover photo: iStock

First printing, 2009

Printed in the United States of America

Scripture quotations are taken from the ESV® Bible (*The Holy Bible: English Standard Version®*). Copyright © 2001 by Crossway. Used by permission. All rights reserved.

ISBN-13: 978-1-4335-0260-6
ISBN-10: 1-4335-0260-7
PDF ISBN: 978-1-4335-0547-8
Mobipocket ISBN: 978-1-4335-0548-5
ePub ISBN: 978-1-4335-2113-3

Library of Congress Cataloging-in-Publication Data
Nichols, Stephen J., 1970–
   Ancient Word, changing worlds : the doctrine of Scripture in a
modern age / Stephen J. Nichols and Eric T. Brandt.
     p. cm.
   Includes bibliographical references.
   ISBN 978-1-4335-0260-6 (tpb)
   1. Bible—Evidences, authority, etc. I. Brandt, Eric T., 1984– . II. Title.
BS480.N48   2009
220.1—dc22   2008040948

Crossway is a publishing ministry of Good News Publishers.

CH		21	20	19	18	17	16	15	14	13	12
16	15	14	13	12	11	10	9	8	7	6	5	4	3

For Heidi
(SJN)

For Megan
(ETB)

Loving wives, cherished friends

CONTENTS

ACKNOWLEDGMENTS

Eric would like to thank Steve for suggesting that they write this book together. He is also grateful to his new bride, Megan, for her support and assistance with this project. He will not easily forget how gracious and encouraging she was as he wrote his last few pages on their honeymoon.

Steve would like to thank his colleagues and administrators at Lancaster Bible College for their commitment to the Word that endures forever. He is also grateful to his wife, Heidi, for reading through his chapters. They are much better off for it.

We are grateful to Lester Hicks, who read an early version of the manuscript and made many helpful observations. Ted Griffin at Crossway once again proved to be a most observant and kind editor. And finally, we are grateful to Al Fisher for both a new and a seasoned friendship.

We dedicate this book to our wives, without whom this book wouldn't have been written.

INTRODUCTION

Mark Twain, as only he could, once said, "It is full of interest. It has noble poetry in it; and some clever fables; and some blood-drenched history; and some good morals; and a wealth of obscenity; and upwards of a thousand lies."[1] Of course, you have figured out that he was speaking of the Bible, otherwise referred to as the Good Book. That book has had its defenders and detractors, champions and critics, friends and foes. Perhaps in no time has the Bible been more a subject of controversy, however, than in the modern age, this age of Mark Twain and of the rise of modern science and of rapid and cataclysmic change.

It seems that each age of the church has its unique challenges and opportunities. The early church faced the crisis of persecution and the crises of the heretics who challenged the biblical teaching on, among other things, Christ. The medieval church wrestled with the union of church and empire. The church in the era of the Reformation not only had to withstand the religious and political establishment but also had to reconstruct the church itself, from the platform planks of significant doctrines all the way to the structure of the church service. The church in the "modern age," a rather ambiguous descriptor, also faces unique challenges and opportunities. Perhaps chief among them is the role of the supernatural in light of the ascendancy of naturalistic and scientific worldviews. To put the matter differently, what does an ancient book, the supernatural revelation from God contained in the pages of Scripture, have to say to an increasingly complex and changing modern world? How does an ancient word speak to our changing world?

In the past eras of the church, various theologians and church

---

[1]Mark Twain, *Letters from the Earth: Uncensored Writings* (New York: Harper Perennial Modern Classics, 2004), 14.

leaders rose to the occasion of the challenges facing the church, leading the church into deeper reflection on Scripture and clearer expression of theology and worship. The Christological heresies of the early church yielded the treasures of the Nicene and Chalcedonian Creeds. The Reformation's recovery of both Scripture and the apostolic teaching produced the Reformation *solas* of *sola scriptura* (Scripture alone), *sola fide* and *sola gratia* (salvation and justification by faith alone and by grace alone), *solus Christus* (Christ alone), and *soli Deo gloria* (for the glory of God alone). And so it is in the modern age. The challenge to supernatural revelation, the challenge to the Bible, has been met with deeper reflection on and clearer expression of the doctrines of Scripture. These doctrines orbit around three words, words that have received a great deal of attention in the nineteenth, twentieth, and now into the twenty-first centuries. These three words are *inspiration*, *inerrancy*, and *interpretation*. This book tells the story of these words, and particularly the story of how these words were developed in these last few centuries. It is the story of how the ancient word of God speaks to and in our changing world.

Chapter 1 begins with the first of these words, *inspiration*, the doctrine that stresses the divine origin of Scripture. Religious writings claim to be the words of the divine. The Bible is not unique in laying forth such a claim. But the Bible claims not simply to be another revelation by another deity. The Bible claims to be the true and authentic word of the one and only Triune God. This claim is out of step with the modern world on two counts. First, it's a claim to the reality and reliability of the supernatural. Secondly, it's an exclusive claim. The first claim is out of step with a naturalistic worldview, while the second is out of step with a pluralistic worldview. Yet, the doctrine of inspiration is foundational to the Christian view of revelation. And since Christians endeavor to build their faith and practice upon Scripture, the doctrine of inspiration arguably plays a central role in all doctrine.

Closely related to the doctrine of inspiration comes the second word this book treats, *inerrancy*. B. B. Warfield, one of the figures who casts a long shadow over this discussion, made the connection to inspiration and inerrancy by simply claiming that if Scripture is inspired, of divine origin, then it follows that it is authoritative, reliable, and true, which is to say inerrant. Now the debate, especially as the twentieth century goes, really heats up. As one book title has it, we have embarked on *The Battle for the Bible*. Is the Bible true? Is it accurate? These questions are fundamental to the Christian faith and the Christian claims.

Just as you cannot speak of the Bible without addressing inspiration and inerrancy, one more word merits attention, *interpretation*. Like inspiration and inerrancy, this word too has drawn a great deal of attention in recent decades. Developments in the fields of linguistics and literary criticism have had quite a ripple effect on biblical interpretation. In some ways, the ascendancy of these fields of linguistics and literary criticism stands behind this new age we have entered into culturally, the postmodern era. Many of the prominent and founding voices of postmodernism, such as Jacques Derrida and Jean-François Lyotard, were primarily literary scholars. These developments and these figures have changed the nature of the discussion of how individuals and communities understand and relate to texts. Interpretation of the biblical text is not immune from these developments. As can be expected, not a little debate has emerged over these developments in the field of biblical interpretation. Indeed, if every age of the church has its unique challenges and opportunities, it does seem that in the modern age, and now in the postmodern age as well, the doctrine of Scripture has been on center stage.

This book looks at each of these words. Chapter 1 relays the narrative of the development of the doctrine of inspiration, chapter 3 treats inerrancy, and chapter 5 explores interpretation. These narrative chapters are complemented by chapters 2, 4, and 6, which provide readings in the primary source documents. These readings present the voices of the major figures in these debates, allowing these figures to speak for themselves. These readings also provide succinct summaries, pointing readers, should you want more, to a whole wealth of material. This book covers roughly a 150-year history, from the 1850s right up until this first decade of the twenty-first century. Of course, these three words—*inspiration*, *inerrancy*, and *interpretation*—continue to garner much interest and are the subject of no little controversy, in days past and recent.

The Bible has a rich history in the modern world. Copies are given away at weddings and births and placed in hotel room nightstands. Hands are placed on it for the taking of oaths. And, as many country songs point out, it is almost ubiquitously regarded as the Good Book. But the Bible also faces its share of attacks and criticism. In the face of those attacks, many biblical scholars and theologians have taken up the challenge of defending and commending the Bible. They have labored to show that an ancient book does indeed have something to say to modern and even postmodern people. This book seeks to tell that story.

SACRED WORD IN THE MODERN WORLD: THE INSPIRATION OF SCRIPTURE

1

We believers in the full inspiration of the Bible do not merely admit that. We insist upon it.

J. GRESHAM MACHEN

I've often thought the Bible should have a disclaimer in the front saying this is fiction.

IAN MCKELLAN

No less than the famed "Lion of Princeton," B. B. Warfield, nearly built a whole career on two words: *inspiration* and *inerrancy*. And from the late nineteenth on into the twentieth centuries, these were fighting words. Some have claimed that Warfield spent so much time with these words because he was a contentious man, that he was always up for a good fight. This portrayal has Warfield on the prowl for some argument that he could win, scouring for some controversy through which he could showcase his theological talents. No doubt, Warfield could handle himself, he could win arguments, and he had plenty of theological ability and mettle to display if he wanted to. But he took up this challenge not because he was a pugilist by nature and not because he belonged to some theological persuasion that relished controversy. Instead, if we take him at his word, he engaged the discussion over these words because they are so crucial to Christianity. Warfield indeed fought for these doctrines, but he fought for them because he knew how important they are to the "doctrine and duty," the thought and practice, of the church.

These two words that occupied so much of Warfield's time and energy, inspiration and inerrancy, are used by theologians to discuss the authority of Scripture, one of, if not the chief of, Scripture's attributes. One way to get at the nature of Scripture is to explore its attributes, which tend to be summed up in a list of four: authority, necessity, clarity, and sufficiency. It might be helpful, though, to add a fifth attribute: *beauty*. Scripture is beautiful. Think of the simple poetry of Psalm 23 or the compelling force of Paul's argument structures or the finely spun narratives in the Old Testament or in the Gospels. Scripture is remarkable as literature, as beautiful literature. Scripture is also *sufficient*, sufficient in relaying the message of redemption, sufficient in laying out all that we need for living the Christian life, and sufficient in proscribing the life and praxis of the church. The gospel message and the fundamental teachings of Scripture are also *clear*. Older works refer to this as the perspicuity of Scripture, perspicuous being a rather complicated word that simply means "clear." You don't need a decoder ring to get the message of Scripture; the message of Scripture is clear. Scripture is also *necessary*. Again, it is necessary in terms of the gospel message and in terms of what God would have us believe about the world he made, about his own self and nature, and even about our own selves and nature.

That brings us to the last attribute of Scripture: *authority*. You could likely make the case that this is the fundamental attribute from which the other four stem. Scripture as authority means that it speaks with solid credibility and legitimacy to all that it addresses. Scripture as authority means that it demands something of its readers, something that other books don't demand. Scripture insists that its readers submit to it. The reason Scripture makes such a unique demand is that it makes a unique claim in reference to its authorship. Scripture claims to be the word of God, to be an inspired text. Scripture's authority derives from its authorship, which leads you back to those two words that Warfield engaged and that dominate the discussion relating to Scripture in the modern world—inspiration and inerrancy. Chapters 3 and 4 take up the discussion of inerrancy; this chapter and the next concern inspiration.

THE CHALLENGE OF THE MODERN AGE

Scripture's unique claim on its readers and its unique authorship make it a bit of a challenging book in the modern age. That's actually an understatement. Scripture's uniqueness is at the heart and center of the challenge it faces in the modern world. In the nineteenth century, Georg Wilhelm Friedrich Hegel introduced a philosophy of history that became quite popular during and after his lifetime. The particular idea is that ideas evolve through a process that he calls the dialectic. One idea dominates the prevailing worldview and outlook, which Hegel called the thesis. A different idea begins to counter that prevailing idea, which Hegel calls the antithesis. Over time and usually involving painful adjustments the two ideas begin to merge, which he terms a synthesis. The new synthesis becomes the thesis, which, you guessed it, eventually faces a new antithesis, and the process continues on and on. Hegel saw this process as always spiraling up, as always making progress.

To illustrate Hegel's theory, consider how Karl Marx applied it to economics. According to Marx, feudalism (the thesis) reigned in the medieval era, followed by capitalism (the antithesis) in the modern era, which then, after battling it out, merged into socialism (the synthesis). Another illustration concerns the one Hegel himself used. The ancient world, Hegel observed, was the mythological age, the age of gods (the thesis). The latter ancient era and the medieval period may be marked as the religious age, the age of the one God (the antithesis). Hegel declared the modern age as the age of science (the synthesis). In Hegel's worldview, there's always progress. It makes no sense whatsoever to look in the rearview mirror. It's silly, infantile, to live in the past. Now comes the application to how the Bible gets perceived in the modern world. The Bible belongs to the past, not to the present. As an ancient book, it does not speak with credibility and legitimacy (authority) to life in the modern world.

The ancients needed myths or religious texts to explain the phenomena they faced. They needed a vehicle to understand storms and suffering, disease and death. Sacred texts, texts claiming to contain the words of God or of the gods, supplied the answers. Moderns, however, have science. Storms are related to gulf streams and weather patterns and water cycles. Diseases come from germs and viruses. Science explains the phenomena, pushing God (religion) or the gods (myth) aside. In Hegel's worldview, one doesn't look back. One just keeps pulsing ahead.

The Bible and the events it records occur in a particular place and time geographically and historically, which is to say the Bible is an ancient book. But the Bible also claims to transcend its age. The Bible as an ancient book speaks to the ancient world, but it also speaks to the medieval world, to the modern age, and even to the postmodern age. The reason? Scripture claims to be more than the words of ancient authors dispensing ancient wisdom for ancient people. The Bible claims to be *inspired*. As such, the Bible lays claim to transcending its age and speaking authoritatively to the modern age, the age of science and of reason.

THE HISTORY OF A WORD

"The word 'inspire' and its derivatives," B. B. Warfield informs us, "seem to have come into Middle English from the French, and have been employed from the first (early in the fourteenth century) in a considerable number of significations, physical and metaphorical, secular and religious." Warfield proceeds to explain one of those religious significations, perhaps the chief one:

> The Biblical books are called inspired as the Divinely determined products of inspired men; the Biblical writers are called inspired as breathed into by the Holy Spirit, so that the product of their activities transcends human powers and becomes Divinely authoritative. Inspiration is, therefore, usually defined as a supernatural influence exerted on the sacred writers by the Spirit of God, by virtue of which their writings are given Divine trustworthiness.[1]

---

[1] B. B. Warfield, "Inspiration," *International Standard Bible Encyclopedia*, 4 vols., ed. James Orr (Chicago: Howard-Severance, 1915), 3:1473.

Then Warfield takes us to 2 Timothy 3:16. This definition of Warfield's and this text that he turns to first become the virtual template for discussing inspiration, though most are not as intrigued by etymology as Warfield was and consequently tend to overlook the French derivation of the English word. Second Timothy 3:16 is a good place to start, for in it Paul uses the Greek word *theopneustos*, translated "inspired" in many English versions. The word, as Warfield's definition informs us, points to the divine origin of the text. While the doctrine of inspiration is well served by starting with 2 Timothy 3:16, the formulation of the doctrine by no means stops there. Second Peter 1:21 also informs us, "For no prophecy was ever produced by the will of man, but men spoke from God as they were carried along by the Holy Spirit." Alongside these two texts, Scripture is replete with its claim to divine authorship. Paul consistently makes the case that the authority of his words does not derive from himself; it derives from his office as apostle, one who has been appointed to speak for God (Gal. 1:11–12).

The Old Testament prophets consistently and widely refer to their role as mouthpieces for God. "Thus says the LORD . . ." is repeated again and again throughout the prophetic books. What makes Christ's own words in the Sermon on the Mount in Matthew 5–7 so striking is the way in which he contrasts himself with the prophets of old. Christ speaks on his own authority. "You have heard that it was said, but I say to you" becomes the refrain punctuating the sermon. The prophets in comparison would never make such a claim. It's not "Hear the word of Isaiah . . . or of Jeremiah . . . or of Malachi." Rather, it is the word of the Lord spoken through the prophet. Scripture consistently and widely claims to be the very words of God.

Throughout church history, this belief in inspiration, the divine origin of Scripture, has been a central hallmark of Christian orthodoxy. In the early church the biblical authors were called *theologians* because they literally spoke (the Greek word *logos* in its verb form means "to speak") for God (the Greek word for God is *Theos*). Moses was a theologian in the truest sense of that word.

The biblical prophets, David, the Gospel writers, Paul, Peter, and the other writers of the New Testament epistles were all theologians. The early church fathers also recognized that because the biblical authors spoke for God, their words carried the weight of authority with them. These early church fathers often wrote their own epistles to the churches under their care, and in these letters they would pass along their advice on all sorts of matters. When, however, they wanted to make a particular point to these churches, they stepped out of the way and quoted the Bible. They didn't defend it; they didn't offer arguments for the authenticity of the text. They just quoted it, revealing the level of authority ascribed to the biblical books in the early church.

The Reformers approached Scripture in the same way. The Reformation, from one angle, can be seen as a debate around Scripture's authority. Either Scripture stands over and above us as individual persons and as the corporate people of God, or we, either as individuals or as the collective body of the church, stand over it. The Reformation plank of *sola scriptura* addresses this directly, proclaiming emphatically and explicitly that Scripture stands over us as individuals and over us as the collective body of Christ. The church's teaching and practice must be derived from its pages or the church risks running afoul. The Reformation was in one sense a debate over authority.

Curiously enough, the Renaissance carried on the same debate over authority with the later medieval Roman Catholic Church. The figures in the Renaissance, like the Reformers, turned away from lodging authority in the ecclesiastical structure. Unlike the Reformation, however, the Renaissance promoted looking within at the human mind or looking without to nature. Eventually, born of those seeds, rationalism and science would flower as the bases for knowledge, as the authority. The Reformers, however, looked past themselves and past nature to the one who created both. They not only looked to the Creator, they also listened to the Creator. They listened to his revelation as the authority.

This can be seen in John Calvin's magisterial *Institutes of the Christian Religion*. Calvin scholar Edward Dowey has made a good case that Calvin's thought can be understood against this Renaissance quest for knowledge in light of the meltdown of the medieval Roman Catholic Church. Consequently, Calvin begins his theology with a discussion of God as Creator who has revealed himself. Revelation is the starting point. It's not just a convenient starting point. According to Calvin, it's the only viable one.[2] Since Calvin, theologians on the side of orthodoxy have realized just how right he was and is.

This high view of Scripture, stemming from the idea of inspiration and divine origin of the text, was not without challenge. The early church fathers contended with those who promoted false books of the Bible, books termed pseudepigrapha. These include books like the Gospel of Thomas or the Gospel of Judas, books that are falsely (*pseudo*) written (*grapha*) in that they are written by later groups who claim to be written by apostles like Thomas. These books are not only faulty because of their authorship but also because of their content. The Reformers, as mentioned above, had to contend with those who tried to hem in the word of God, circumscribing it with tradition. This gets to the heart of Luther's efforts at reform. He saw the word bound to the church and not the other way around.

The Reformers also battled the loss of the word. Widespread illiteracy, not to mention the powers of superstition, had captivated much of the laity. Copies of the Bible were extremely scarce, and then only in Latin, the language of a privileged few. William Tyndale expressed the Reformation opposition best in his herculean efforts to bring the Bible into print in the language of the people.

CHANGING ATTITUDES

Neglect, abuse, distortion—these were the culprits over the centuries that weakened the level of authority that people both inside and

---

[2]Edward A. Dowey Jr., *The Knowledge of God in Calvin's Theology* (Grand Rapids, MI: Eerdmans, 1974); John Calvin, *Institutes of the Christian Religion*, Book I.

outside the church ascribed to the Bible. The modern age, however, introduced a new culprit, one that might just be a bit more pernicious: the judgment of the Bible's irrelevance. The Bible in the modern world is sort of like a long-term employee who is about to get sacked. The employee is called into the manager's office to be told what wonderful contributions he's made to the company in the past. He's told what great qualities he has, what a fine person he is. Then he's told that his department is being restructured, that he is redundant. All of which is interpreted as saying, you are no longer needed or wanted. The Bible was good at one time but is outmoded and can't keep up with the times. Or so goes the judgment of the modern age.

Mark Noll once wrote, "On the face of it, it would be hard to imagine a nation more thoroughly biblical than the United States between the American Revolution and the Civil War."[3] His opening phrase, "On the face of it," is instructive. The reigning attitude toward the Bible in American culture was not that it was the Truth, but that it was the Story that provided the backbone for the American story. Nevertheless, Noll makes the case that the Bible had a presumed prominence up to America's War Between the States. Post-Civil War America is another story. This is the story of how the Bible, like that longtime employee, got sacked.

In the cold Boston winter months of 1891, Harvard professor Joseph Henry Thayer presented a lecture that would later be published under the title *The Change of Attitude Towards the Bible*. Thayer's first line reveals that he is hesitant, and for good reason. He's about to articulate what all of his colleagues are thinking, and he realizes that what he and they are thinking is dangerous. By saying what he's about to say, he risks "forfeiting" the "general approval of his fellow Christians." To stem off the forfeiture, he pleads his *bona fides* as a Christian scholar and gentleman. Then he proceeds to say what he wants to say.

Thayer begins with the "Reformed or Calvinistic" view of

---

[3]Mark A. Noll, "The Image of the United States as a Biblical Nation, 1776–1865," *The Bible In America: Essays in Cultural History*, ed. Nathan O. Hatch and Mark A. Noll (New York: Oxford University Press, 1982), 39.

Scripture, which is his not so veiled way of referring to Warfield and the Princetonians, a constellation of biblical scholars and theologians at Princeton Theological Seminary from the 1850s until the 1920s including Charles Hodge, his son A. A. Hodge, B. B. Warfield, and J. Gresham Machen. The Princetonian view "has laid a disproportionate emphasis on the full and final character of the Scriptural teaching relative to the whole range of speculation and conduct, life and destiny." This is Thayer's way of expressing the view of verbal, plenary inspiration. This view, given full expression by Charles Hodge in 1857, contends that all (*plenary* means "full" or "entire") of the words (*verbal*) of the Bible are from God. Thayer continues, observing that this view, held by "a certain class of rough and ready controversialists," "furnishes" them "with a bludgeon which they are prone to mistake for the sword of the Lord." Again, that "certain class" would indeed be Warfield and the Princetonians, caricatured as always trolling for a good fight. The Princetonian view, Thayer continues, was "comparatively harmless in bygone days." Now it has "become a yoke." Here's why:

> But by reason of improved methods of philological study, of progress in science and discovery, of accumulating results in archaeological and historic [sic] research, the theory has come to occasion restlessness and perplexity, at times not a little distress, in thoughtful souls. It has become a yoke which they—unlike their fathers—are unable to bear.[4]

This quotation deserves unpacking. "Improved methods of philological study" is a reference to higher criticism, the upshot of which is to see the Bible as a significantly human book. "Progress in science" refers to what the above pages outlined. The scientific worldview of moderns is not the same as the mythological worldview of the ancients. Progress means that you don't go back. Thayer does not outline the archaeological or historical research he alludes to, but he's likely referring to the gaps in the archaeo-

---

[4]Joseph Henry Thayer, *The Change of Attitude Towards the Bible* (Boston: Houghton, Mifflin, and Company, 1891), 10–11.

logical record concerning biblical events. All of this is enough to make a "thoughtful" person blush in embarrassment. To borrow from a car commercial a few years back, the Princetonian view of Scripture was your father's view. This new generation needs a new view, a view that's not that of their fathers. It is also important to note what Thayer does not advocate. He does not advocate turning away from Scripture altogether or even in the main. He just wants a milder view, one that allows for some fuzzy boundaries and wiggle room—one that's not so distressful to thoughtful souls. This is the new view of Scripture that Thayer commends.

Between the American Civil War and the beginnings of the twentieth century, attitudes toward the Bible had changed indeed. These new attitudes brought about a whole new set of categories: *modernists*, those who saw no need for keeping the ancient book of the Bible or for keeping the religion it spawned; *liberals*, those who wanted to keep the ancient book of the Bible and Christianity but needed to retool both to fall in line with modern sensibilities; and *fundamentalists*, those who thought the Bible was as true in all of its particulars for moderns as it was for ancients. Admittedly, *fundamentalism* is a complicated term, meaning different things to different people at different times. The term does serve well, though, to describe theological conservatives who held to a high view of Scripture during the decades roughly from the 1890s through the 1930s.

THE LION'S DEN

These theological conservatives, especially when it came to the doctrine of Scripture, had found a home at Princeton and had a de facto leader in Benjamin B. Warfield, affectionately dubbed "The Lion of Princeton." Born in the South in 1851, Warfield first began his academic career at Western Seminary near Pittsburgh before moving on to Princeton in 1887. He was returning to his alma mater, having studied there under Charles Hodge. Charles Hodge passed the mantle on to his son A. A. Hodge. After A. A. Hodge's death in 1886, the mantle passed to Warfield. Warfield not only studied at Princeton, he also spent a year studying overseas in Europe. By 1887 he had already published a number of significant works and had quite a reputation. He was poised, in other words, to carry on Princeton's role in defending and commending the authority of the Bible and its supernatural worldview.

Warfield's role in the Bible's defense actually predates his return to Princeton as a professor. In 1881 he and A. A. Hodge coauthored an article for *The Presbyterian Review* simply titled "Inspiration." Charles Hodge had first written on the topic in 1857. Since then, however, new challenges to the doctrine had arisen. The new challenges orbited around higher criticism and those recent developments in philology mentioned in Thayer's lecture. The activity of higher criticism analyzes the Bible in order to determine its authorship and historicity. This analysis consists of unraveling the various literary sources underlying the biblical books. Higher criticism can take the shape of "form criticism," which looks for literary units marked off by a particular form or pattern. It can also take the shape of "tradition criticism," which looks for literary units that adhere to a certain tradition or a certain set of beliefs and understanding.

Whichever approach, higher criticism starts with the presupposition that the Bible or even particular books of the Bible are composites, made up of various strands. From the perspective of higher criticism, authors of biblical books function more like editors who cleverly and creatively weave the strands, coming from a variety of sources, together. Advocates of higher criticism see their task as teasing the strands apart. The two main areas of the Bible that received a great deal of attention by higher critics in the nineteenth century were the Pentateuch, the first five books of the Old Testament ascribed to Moses, and the four New Testament Gospels. The upshot of this higher criticism, or to use a term by Roy A. Harrisville and Walter Sundberg, "rationalist biblical criticism," is to see the Bible and its books not as the product of divine agency but as the product of human endeavors.

Consider higher criticism and the Pentateuch. Various higher critics had identified four authorial strands: the Yahwist, the Elohist, the Deuteronimist, and the Priestly strand. These strands were identified by the four initials J-E-D-P. Building on this, Julius Wellhausen argued in his *History of Israel* (1878) that much of the Pentateuch comes from the time after the exile and that Moses certainly was not the author. The Pentateuch is more about the beliefs of these four groups than it is an accurate and reliable revelation from God.

Similar attacks came against the Gospels. While higher criticism of the Gospels stretches back to the eighteenth century, David Friedrich Strauss took it to new heights (or depths?) with the publication of his *Life of Jesus* in 1835. This set off a virtual cottage industry of scholars on a quest for the historical Jesus. The historical Jesus, as this approach has it, lies buried somewhere in the texts of the Gospels, which were more concerned with the Jesus of faith, the fictitious Jesus who was a creation of various Christian communities who had attached names of the apostles to their own books. According to the scholars questing after Jesus, the Bible is viewed as a book of faith, not to be taken for granted as historically reliable. As with the Pentateuch, the Gospels are more about the beliefs of the communities that produced them than they are an accurate and reliable revelation of Christ from God.

On the one side of biblical scholarship in the nineteenth century were these higher critics or rationalists who were committed to the presupposition that the Bible is a human book. On the other side were those committed to the presupposition that the Bible is the word of God. To put the matter directly, either the Bible is a supernatural book (the orthodox view) or it is a natural book (the higher or rationalist criticism view). The rationalist criticism view nearly dominated European biblical studies in the nineteenth century. By 1881 young Warfield saw it as a burgeoning problem in America. In attempts to stem it off, he proposed the article to one of the editors of *The Presbyterian Review*, A. A. Hodge, who decided to sign on as a cowriter.[5]

---

[5]For a history of European rationalist criticism, see Roy A. Harrisville and Walter Sundberg, *The Bible in Modern Culture: Baruch Spinoza to Brevard Childs* (Grand Rapids, MI: Eerdmans, 2002).

Probably neither Hodge nor Warfield had any idea what controversy this article would cause, both then and now. As for the controversies then, this article was the first in what would be a series of eight articles in *The Presbyterian Review* on the topics of inspiration and biblical criticism. The writer of two of those articles and also an editor of *The Presbyterian Review*, Charles A. Briggs, would face heresy trials for his views in his denomination, the Presbyterian Church USA, in the 1890s. Briggs will factor more significantly in the story of inerrancy in chapters 3 and 4, but for now it suffices to say that Briggs could not countenance the view of inspiration laid out by Hodge and Warfield in their article. More recently, Jack Rogers and Donald McKim have taken issue with the view as well, in their 1979 book *The Authority and Interpretation of the Bible: An Historical Approach*. The so-called Rogers/McKim proposal has Hodge and Warfield inventing the modern evangelical view of verbal, plenary inspiration and a concomitant view of inerrancy. This particular view ran perniciously through fundamentalism, from the ivy-strewn halls of Princeton Seminary to the pages of Harold Lindsell's *Battle for the Bible* (1976). Rogers and McKim argued for another view, which they understood to be held by the biblical authors and by the leading lights of church history from Augustine on through the Reformers. The Princetonians had created the doctrine of verbal plenary inspiration and inerrancy *ex nihilo*. The Rogers/McKim proposal points to a less exacting view of inspiration and a more flexible view of inerrancy, which restricts inerrancy to matters of faith only.

Even more recently, Stanley Grenz contended that while the Princetonians were not as revisionist as Rogers and McKim made them out to be, their particular emphasis on inspiration was far too much. Grenz counters, "We can no longer construct our doctrine of Scripture in the classical manner," with the Princetonians holding the honor of the classical manner. Even Islamic websites will cite the Hodge and Warfield article when speaking of the

Christian view of plenary inspiration. Did Hodge and Warfield have any idea of the firestorm of controversy they were setting off with their article or how widely distributed it would be? They certainly couldn't foresee being cited on Islamic websites. But they are. The sheer controversy surrounding this article is enough to warrant a close look at it. The article takes its place as one of the most significant texts in the formation of the orthodox view of the authority of Scripture.[6]

Figure 1.1
Inspiration Timeline

1857	Charles Hodge publishes "Inspiration."
1881	A. A. Hodge and B. B. Warfield coauthor "Inspiration" in *The Presbyterian Review.*
1881	Charles A. Briggs publishes "Critical Theories of the Sacred Scriptures" in *The Presbyterian Review* in response to Hodge and Warfield.
1887	B. F. Westcott publishes *Introduction to the Study of the Gospels.*
1888	Basil Manly publishes *The Bible Doctrine of Inspiration.*
1889	Robert F. Horton publishes *Inspiration and the Bible.*
1891	Briggs gives inaugural address at Union Seminary, "The Authority of Holy Scripture."
1891	Joseph Henry Thayer publishes *The Change of Attitude Towards the Bible.*
1892	PCUSA General Assembly issues Portland Deliverance.
1893	Briggs is suspended from the PCUSA.
1910	James Orr publishes *Revelation and Inspiration.*
1910	PCUSA General Assembly adopts the "Five Point Deliverance."
1910–1915	*The Fundamentals* are published in twelve volumes, edited by R. A. Torrey, A. C. Dixon, and others.
1915	Warfield publishes articles on revelation and inspiration in Orr's *International Standard Bible Encyclopedia.*
1922	Harry Emerson Fosdick preaches "Shall the Fundamentalists Win?"
1923	J. Gresham Machen publishes *Christianity and Liberalism.*
1925	PCUSA drops "Five Point Deliverance."
1958	J. I. Packer publishes *"Fundamentalism" and the Word of God.*
1963	Dewey M. Beegle publishes *The Inspiration of Scripture.*
1966	G. C. Berkouwer publishes *Holy Scripture* (English translation in 1975).

---

[6]For a discussion of the 1881 Hodge and Warfield article, see Mark A. Noll, *The Princeton Theology 1812–1921: Scripture, Science, and Theological Method from Archibald Alexander to Benjamin Breckinridge Warfield* (Grand Rapids, MI: Baker Academic, 2001), 218–231; Jack Rogers and Donald McKim, *The Authority and Interpretation of the Bible: An Historical Approach* (New York: Harper, 1979); Stanley Grenz, *Revisioning Evangelical Theology: A Fresh Agenda for the 21st Century* (Downers Grove, IL: InterVarsity Press, 1993), 116.

VERBAL, PLENARY INSPIRATION (AND WHY IT MATTERS)

The Hodge and Warfield article starts by expressing a particular definition and use of the term *inspiration*. They are not talking about a generic inspiration or about influence but about inspiration in a "fixed and narrow sense." The closest synonym they offer is superintendence, adding, "This superintendence attended the entire process of the genesis of Scripture, and particularly the process of the final composition of the record." This superintendence also includes "historic processes and the concurrence of natural and supernatural forces." They conclude that this superintendence results in "the absolute infallibility of the record . . . in the original autograph." By speaking of concurrence with the human authors, Hodge and Warfield acknowledge that the verbal, plenary view does not allow for the dictation theory or a mechanical view of inspiration. In the dictation view, the biblical authors might as well be in a trance as God takes over. Hodge and Warfield's view allows for the personality and even the idiosyncrasies of the biblical authors to shine (or in some cases glare) through.[7]

After giving the definition of inspiration, three presuppositions are set out. First, inspiration is put in its place, which is to say that Hodge and Warfield acknowledge that while inspiration is true, "it is not in the first instance a principle fundamental to the truth of the Christian religion." In a later article on inspiration, Warfield would say, "We found the whole system of Christian doctrine on plenary inspiration as little as we found it upon the doctrine of angelic existences."[8] This doesn't mean they downplayed the doctrine, but it is important to see this qualification.

In the second presupposition, they observe that inspiration "must be conditioned upon our general views of God's relation to the world, and his methods of influencing the souls of men." This is their way of expressing the difference between supernaturalistic

[7] A. A. Hodge and B. B. Warfield, "Inspiration," *The Presbyterian Review* 2 (April 1881), 225–260. The following quotations, unless otherwise noted, are from this article.
[8] B. B. Warfield, "The Real Problem of Inspiration," *The Presbyterian and Reformed Review*, 4 (1893), 177–221.

and naturalistic worldviews. They express this directly: "The only really dangerous opposition to the church doctrine of inspiration comes either directly or indirectly, but always ultimately, from some false view of God's relation to the world, of his methods of working, and of the possibility of a supernatural agency penetrating and altering the course of a natural process." This leads to the third presupposition, the "continuity between all the various provinces and methods of God's working." Each of these, the supernatural and the natural, God and the human authors, constitute "one system in the execution of one plan," with "all these agents and all these methods [being] so perfectly adjusted and controlled . . . [that] all together infallibly bring about the result God designs." This is the notion of concursus. Warfield offers a fuller discussion of concursus in his essay "The Divine and Human in the Bible," published in *The Presbyterian Review* in 1894.

After setting out these three presuppositions, Hodge and Warfield turn next to the genesis of Scripture, again returning to the idea of the human agency in the writing of Scripture. Such human agency is "everywhere apparent, and gives substance and form to the entire collection of writings." This means in short that the Scriptures have been generated "through an historic process," with the Holy Spirit ever present throughout the process. Then they put forward their definition of inspiration as plenary, verbal inspiration, anticipating various objections or alternative views to the claim of verbal inspiration. The first is that to some the verbal theory sounds like the dictation theory. They dispense with that handily. The second is an alternative to verbal inspiration that instead pictures the biblical authors as inspired in a general way who then set out to write in their own abilities and limitations of divine truth, resulting in an adequate but not infallible text. A third objection also puts forth an alternative view, claiming that "while the thoughts of the sacred writers concerning doctrine and duty were inspired and errorless, their language was of purely human suggestion, and more or less accurate." Yet another view sees the biblical authors as inspired and therefore inerrant when it comes to matters of faith and practice or of matters pertaining to "doctrine and duty," but not so when it comes to matters of history or science or geography and the like. These elements of the Bible are deemed of secondary importance and contain inaccuracies and discrepancies. In reply, Hodge and Warfield assert, "the Scriptures not only contain, but *are, the word of God*" (emphasis theirs).

So far much of the article has been on the side of definition and assertion. In the next sections of the article, Hodge and Warfield offer proofs and evidence. They start with the text of Scripture itself and its self-claims. The New Testament authors "continually assert" that the Old Testament is the word of God. The apostles, the writers of the New Testament, also consistently claim to speak for God. Hodge and Warfield next point to Scripture's congruity despite its having so many human authors over such a long stretch of time. They also refer to the work of others who demonstrate Scripture's compatibility with the natural sciences. Finally, they turn to church history, running through the litany of those from the church fathers on down through the Reformers who held to Scripture as the very words of God. They reach the following conclusion concerning the inspired and inerrant text: "This has been from the first the general faith of the historical church and of the Bible-loving, spiritual people of God. The very letter of the word has been proved from ancient times to be a tremendous power in human life."

Having said all this, Hodge and Warfield can now turn to the issue of criticism, the section of the essay entitled "Critical Objections Tried." After this essay, Warfield returned to the subject of critical objections and responses again and again. In summarizing his contributions here, a number of things can be noted. First, Warfield does not advocate a naive view of inspiration or of biblical studies and scholarship. Warfield was well schooled in the difficulties and problems the text presents to biblical scholars. He was well aware of discrepancies in the biblical narrative, be they the different numbers given in Old Testament accounts or problems of harmonizing the Synoptic Gospels. He was well aware of the problems of textual criticism. Scholars sometimes refer to this as "lower criticism," the challenge of the differences between manuscripts of the Bible in the original documents. Warfield wrote a book on textual criticism and was so bold as to publish an article showing why the longer ending of Mark (Mark 16:9–20) is inauthentic and should be discarded. He even admits that this means "we have an incomplete document in Mark's Gospel." What's more, Warfield published this article in the very conservative and very fundamentalist *Sunday School Times*. Moisés Silva, himself a rather prominent New Testament scholar, has come to the conclusion that Warfield has espoused anything but a naive view of inspiration, adding, "The contemporary debate regarding inerrancy appears hopelessly vitiated by the failure—in both conservative and nonconservative camps—to mark how carefully nuanced were Warfield's formulations."[9]

Warfield offers a succinct treatment of the challenges raised by higher criticism in his 1894 article in *The Presbyterian Review*, "The Divine and Human in the Bible." The Bible is fully and entirely human and fully and entirely divine continuously and harmoniously. This again is Warfield's doctrine of concursus. Warfield puts it this way: the Bible is "a divine-human book in which every word is at once divine and human." Ignoring this in either direction, Warfield observes, ends in disaster.

From the end of the Civil War until the turn of the twentieth century, American attitudes toward the Bible had changed. And in the midst of all the flux, the Princetonians were simply not ready to give up on the authority of the Bible without an argument. They offered a carefully nuanced but firm doctrine of inspiration, that of verbal, plenary inspiration. But, as to be expected, not all saw it the same way.

[9]B. B. Warfield, "The Genuineness of Mark 16:9–20," *Sunday School Times* 24, No. 48 (December 2, 1882): 755–756; Moisés Silva, "Old Princeton, Westminster, and Inerrancy," *Inerrancy and Hermeneutic: A Tradition, a Challenge, a Debate*, ed. Harvie M. Conn (Grand Rapids, MI: Baker, 1988), 68–69.

THE SHEKINAH FROM THE SHRINE

While Charles Briggs disagreed with Hodge and Warfield, he certainly did not go as far in his disagreement with them as would Harry Emerson Fosdick. Fosdick had a wide following, preaching in large churches, speaking to massive audiences on the radio, and writing best-selling books. Behind all of that popular speaking and writing was a well-trained and very clever mind. While the fundamentalists were digging in their heels and looking at best outdated and at worst mean-spirited, Fosdick finessed his audiences, and they, by the tens of thousands, listened. To win them over, he proposed what amounted to a new religion, one that had the skeleton of Christianity but with a fresh face and body acceptable to moderns. He knew the power of words and used those words to proffer a new view of the Bible and a new Christianity.

Fosdick could turn a phrase; so he spoke of "the Shekinah distinguished from the shrine." He wanted the "Gospel freed from its entanglements." On the surface this may sound good, but digging a little deeper reveals that the shrine and entanglements that Fosdick refers to are nothing else but the Bible. The Bible in its form is the shrine, but inside it, if we get past the particulars, we are led to the abiding truths. The words are historic, but underlying those words is the abiding sense. The beauty of liberalism and modern sensibilities, Fosdick argues, is that they offer "intellectual liberation from an old literalism" and consequently "incalculable spiritual enrichment" for moderns. Fosdick, who retooled Scripture so it could better speak to human needs, transformed the sermon into therapy.[10]

By the time Fosdick was in full swing, Archibald Alexander Hodge had long since died.

Benjamin Breckinridge Warfield too had passed. But the mantle they bore had not fallen by the way altogether. It had been picked up by J. Gresham Machen. Actually Warfield essentially placed it on Machen just before he died. Machen, perhaps a little reluctant, was nevertheless well qualified for the task. Like Fosdick, Machen knew

---

[10]Harry Emerson Fosdick, *The Modern Use of the Bible* (New York: Macmillan, 1924), 272–273.

his way around words. He had also been well trained at Princeton and at Germany. But unlike Fosdick, Machen did not see the teaching of Scripture and historic creeds as cause to blush. He didn't look for the abiding truths hidden on the surface of the historic words of the text.[11]

Machen offered a full reply to Fosdick in *Christianity and Liberalism* (1923). In sum, Machen charges that Fosdick's view of authority boils down to individual experience. According to Machen, one's view of inspiration and consequently of the text of the Bible itself has to do with one's starting point. If you start with the supposition that God has revealed himself in all of the words of Scripture, then you submit to the teachings of Scripture, however hard they may be for a modern person or however seemingly challenging they are. If you start with the legitimacy of modern sensibilities, then you can conveniently overlook and downplay those difficult elements. Machen did not deny Fosdick the right to his view of Scripture. Machen just had problems with Fosdick claiming that his view was Christian.

WHAT'S BARTH GOT TO DO WITH IT?

Fosdick had packaged German liberalism for American popular audiences. In the main, he was quite comfortable with such liberalism. Not so with Karl Barth. Barth felt that the old liberalism, in which he had been schooled, suffered two fatal flaws: it didn't preach well, and it was too tame. The old liberalism didn't preach well because it taught biblical interpreters to tease out the strands of authorship. One is left with a dissected text, with pieces strewn about. How one goes from that to a meaningful sermon is a difficult (if not impossible) task indeed. Barth also thought liberalism's view of the Bible to be too tame. The Bible was domesticated or gentrified, made more palatable to modern tastes.

---

[11]For the Warfield and Machen connection, see Stephen J. Nichols, "'The Vital Processes of Controversy': Warfield, Machen, and Fundamentalism," in *B. B. Warfield: Essays on His Life and Thought*, ed. Gary L. W. Johnson (Phillipsburg, NJ: P&R, 2007), 169–194; see also Stephen J. Nichols, *J. Gresham Machen: A Guided Tour of His Life and Thought* (Phillipsburg, NJ: P&R, 2004).

Instead, Barth advocated a position that has the Bible encountering us, standing over us. There is central to Barth's view of Scripture the notion of mystery. It is a mystery how the living God confronts us in the human words of the text. It is this mystery that is missing in liberalism. It is also this mystery that causes Barth to be suspect in the minds of orthodox biblical scholars and theologians, especially on the American side of the Atlantic. Barth's view of inspiration stops short of ascribing the finished product, the sixty-six books of the Bible, as inspired. Instead inspiration is a more active dynamic in Barth. Donald Bloesch, sympathetic to Barth, observes, "For Barth inspiration rests on God's decision to speak his Word ever and again in the history of the church and throughout the text of the Bible."[12] Again, it is this dynamic understanding of inspiration that gave Barth a bad reputation among conservative American theologians such as Carl F. H. Henry, Cornelius Van Til, and Charles C. Ryrie. All three weighed Barth's view and found it wanting.

These days, however, there is a change toward Barth in American evangelical circles. The chilly reception of a generation ago has been exchanged for more welcoming treatments. We are likely too close to see how this paradigm shift will fully impact the American evangelical doctrine of Scripture. For now, however, it is likely safe to venture two comments. One is that it is highly likely that Warfield and the Princetonians will not feature so prominently vis-à-vis Barth. Barth has moved from the margins to a place at the center. He has moved from being a figure who is at best suspect to becoming one who is well-regarded. Secondly, and building on this paradigm shift, evangelical doctrines of Scripture will likely shift toward the Barthian understanding of inspiration. The Barthian view moves away from emphasizing and focusing on a static view of the text toward a more dynamic view of the text. Inspiration is more of a dynamic concept, something that happens as the word is proclaimed in the living Christian community of the church. This latter point reflects a broader epistemological shift occurring

---

[12]Donald G. Bloesch, *Holy Scripture: Revelation, Inspiration, and Interpretation* (Downers Grove, IL: InterVarsity Press, 1994), 103.

culturally from a more objectivist epistemology of modernity to a more community-based epistemology of postmodernism. The work of John Franke and the late Stanley Grenz indicates that this may become more the case for evangelical doctrines of Scripture. Again, time will tell.

CONCLUSION

It is not too much of a stretch to say that the Princetonians, that constellation of biblical scholars and theologians at Princeton Theological Seminary including Charles Hodge, his son A. A. Hodge, B. B. Warfield, and J. Gresham Machen, gave more thought to the expression of the doctrine of inspiration than at any other moment in the life of the church. They bequeathed to the twentieth century the fully formulated doctrine of the verbal, plenary inspiration of Scripture. They forged this doctrine in the cauldrons of controversy, against those who preferred a more natural explanation of the origin and genesis of the Bible. Liberalism attempted a middle way, desiring to be at home with modernity and to have Christianity too. By the middle of the twentieth century, yet another view was fast approaching, that of Karl Barth. While Barth certainly doesn't sound like Harry Emerson Fosdick, neither does he sound like B. B. Warfield. Barth's view of inspiration would dominate the closing decades of the twentieth century and on to the present time. His view also engendered and continues to engender discussions of inerrancy, which according to Warfield and the Princetonians is the necessary correlate of the doctrine of verbal, plenary inspiration and is the subject of chapters 3 and 4.

Addressing the positive advances of biblical studies in the nineteenth century, Warfield also observed that "It has not been a century of quiet and undisturbed study of the Bible. Fierce controversies have raged throughout its whole length." He was speaking from personal experience, at least in reference to the latter decades of the nineteenth century. Then Warfield adds, "But fierce controversies can rage only where strong convictions burn. And amid, or rather by means of, all these controversies knowledge has increased." Warfield had learned to place his confidence in Scripture. After all, as he quips, "The Bible has emerged from these fires, as out of all others, without so much the smell of smoke upon its very garments." Warfield held a strong conviction in the word of God because he knew it to be the word of God, the inspired text of Scripture. Warfield concludes his article, written for the *Homiletical Review* in March 1900, with this look ahead to the next century: "It is the whole Bible that is committed to the twentieth century—to receive from it, as we believe, an even deeper reverence and an even completer obedience."[13]

As the twentieth century moved in, controversies over this ancient book in the modern world by no means abated. Challenges would roll in like the shore's relentless waves. Of course, the names would change, as would the exact nature and contours of the controversy, but underlying that change, the constant of the challenge of the modern world remained. The term *inerrancy* would come to the fore. Those who held to it with strong convictions would encounter those who preferred alternatives. Those who revered the Bible deeply and sought to obey it, as Warfield predicted, would also find that there are those who would just as soon move away from the Bible or those who, while professing to revere it on the one hand, subtly dismantle it on the other. If the nineteenth-century history of Scripture in America was a tale of both strong convictions and fierce controversies, so too would be the story of the twentieth century.

It is worthwhile, though, to pause over inspiration for a moment. Inspiration demands something of the modern and now postmodern world. It demands that we look beyond ourselves and beyond our own experience. It demands in the end that we submit to it. This can be difficult and humbling for someone of any era, but for whatever reason it seems to be especially difficult for those of us in the twenty-

---

[13]B. B. Warfield, "The Century's Progress in Biblical Knowledge," reprinted in *Benjamin B. Warfield, Selected Shorter Writings,* 2 vols., ed. John H. Meeter (Phillipsburg, NJ: P&R, 1970, 1973), 2:13.

first century. Perhaps it is because we have accomplished so much and have gone so far in unlocking our world. Consequently, for all of us, Christians and non-Christians, it is helpful to remember that despite our accomplishments and despite our progress, we may not have all of the answers.

2

The following excerpts from several essays and texts portray the content and the tenor of the debate over the inspiration of Scripture in the modern age. The dispute raged its hottest from the middle of the nineteenth century to the middle of the twentieth. It diminished considerably as the contention over inerrancy and interpretation increased.[1] At its peak, however, the discussion engaged theologians across Europe (especially in Germany), England, and America.[2] This chapter serves as an introduction to the various viewpoints and peculiarities in the inspiration debate, offering concise readings from the major figures who contributed to the development of the doctrine of inspiration. Where it is helpful, a brief explanatory introduction to the selection supplies historical and theological background information.

SOURCES ON INSPIRATION

These are listed in the order of quotation in this chapter.

Charles Hodge, "Inspiration."

A. A. Hodge and B. B. Warfield, "Inspiration."

---

[1]Several worthy treatments from a variety of perspectives on inspiration written within the last three decades include: William J. Abraham, *The Divine Inspiration of Holy Scripture* (New York: Oxford University Press, 1981); I. Howard Marshall, *Biblical Inspiration* (England: Hodder and Stoughton, 1982); Donald G. Bloesch, *Holy Scripture: Revelation, Inspiration, and Interpretation* (Downers Grove, IL: InterVarsity Press, 1994); Paul J. Achtemeier, *Inspiration and Authority: Nature and Function of Christian Scripture*, rev. ed. (Peabody, MA: Hendrickson, 1999); Clark H. Pinnock and Barry L. Callen, *The Scripture Principle: Reclaiming the Full Authority of the Bible* (Grand Rapids, MI: Baker, 2006).

[2]One of the early extensive works on inspiration came from Swiss pastor and theologian Louis Gaussen (1790–1863). Published under several titles, one of the most recent is *The Divine Inspiration of Scripture* (Ross-shire, Scotland: Christian Focus, 2007).

C. A. Briggs, "Critical Theories of the Sacred Scriptures in Relation to Their Inspiration."

B. F. Westcott, *Introduction to the Study of the Gospels.*

Basil Manly, *The Bible Doctrine of Inspiration: Explained and Vindicated.*

Robert F. Horton, *Inspiration and the Bible.*

B. B. Warfield, "Inspiration."

James M. Gray, "The Inspiration of the Bible—Definition, Extent and Proof."

Harry Emerson Fosdick, *The Modern Use of the Bible.*

J. Gresham Machen, *Christianity and Liberalism.*

W. A. Criswell, *Why I Preach That the Bible Is Literally True.*

Karl Barth, *Church Dogmatics*, Vol. 1.2, *The Doctrine of the Word of God.*

G. C. Berkouwer, *Holy Scripture.*

Gordon R. Lewis, "The Human Authorship of Inspired Scripture."

PLENARY AND VERBAL INSPIRATION

After reviewing a book of lectures on the inspiration of Scripture, Charles Hodge felt compelled to write a substantial article on the doctrine. For him, this was no purely academic endeavor. As he writes in the opening lines, "the inspiration of the Scriptures is so connected with faith in Christ, that the latter in a measure necessitates the former." In the excerpt below, Hodge outlines the Princeton view on inspiration, affirming the authority of a God-breathed word and defending both the plenary and verbal aspects of inspiration.

Charles Hodge, "Inspiration" (1857)

In saying that the Bible is the word of God, we mean that he is its author, that he says whatever the Bible says; that everything which the Bible affirms to be true is true; that whatever it says is right is right, and whatever it declares to be wrong is wrong, because its declarations as to truth and duty, as to facts and principles, are the declarations of God. What the Scriptures teach is to be believed, not on the authority of Moses or the prophets, or of the apostles and evangelists, but on the authority of God, who used the sacred writers as his organs of communication. The Bible is the product of one mind. It is one book. . . . [E]verything in the Bible which purports to be the word of God, or which is uttered by those whom he used as his messengers, is to be received with the same faith and submission, as though spoken directly by the lips of God himself. This is the doctrine of plenary, as opposed to the theory of partial, inspiration. . . .

Verbal inspiration, therefore, or that influence of the Spirit which controlled the sacred writers in the selection of their words, allowed them perfect freedom within the limits of truth. They were kept from error, and guided to the use of words which expressed the mind of the Spirit, but within these limits they were free to use such language, and to narrate such circumstances as suited their own taste or purposes.[3]

THE HUMAN AND THE DIVINE IN THE BIBLE

A. A. Hodge and B. B. Warfield wrote the first in a series of eight essays by various authors on the doctrine of inspiration that appeared in *The Presbyterian Review* from 1881 to 1883. In their article the authors defend the essence of Charles Hodge's view on inspiration, strengthening those points that they considered weak and clarifying what was lacking. This selection from Hodge and Warfield outlines something that did not receive due attention in Charles Hodge's article, namely, the interaction of the human and the divine in the formation of Scripture.[4] The second essay in *The Presbyterian Review* series and the second excerpt below was writ-

[3]Charles Hodge, "Inspiration," *Biblical Repertory and Princeton Review* 29 (October 1857): 663–664, 678.
[4]For a more detailed treatment of this subject, see Warfield's 1894 essay, "The Divine and the Human in the Bible," reprinted in *Selected Shorter Writings*, 2 vols., ed. John E. Meeter (Phillipsburg, NJ: P&R, 1970, 1973), 2:542–548, and in Mark Noll, *Princeton Theology, 1812–1921: Scripture, Science, and Theological Method from Archibald Alexander to Benjamin Breckinridge Warfield* (Grand Rapids, MI: Baker, 1983, 2001), 275–279.

ten by C. A. Briggs. In it he hails Hodge and Warfield's article as
such an excellent treatise on the subject that he has only to build
upon it. However, in seeking to build on their work, Briggs also tries
to take it apart. In his passage below, he disagrees with the position
Hodge and Warfield propounded on verbal inspiration (which in
large measure echoed Charles Hodge's view).

A. A. Hodge and B. B. Warfield, "Inspiration" (1881)

The human agency, both in the histories out of which the
Scriptures sprang, and in their immediate composition and inscrip-
tion, is everywhere apparent, and gives substance and form to the
entire collection of writings. It is not merely in the matter of verbal
expression or literary composition that the personal idiosyncrasies of
each author are freely manifested by the untrammeled play of all his
faculties, but the very substance of what they write is evidently for the
most part the product of their own mental and spiritual activities. . . .
As the general characteristic of all their work, each writer was put to
that special part of the general work for which he alone was adapted
by his original endowments, education, special information, and
providential position. Each drew from the stores of his own original
information, from the contributions of other men, and from all other
natural sources. Each sought knowledge, like all other authors, from
the use of his own natural faculties of thought and feeling, of intu-
ition and of logical inference, of memory and imagination, and of
religious experience. Each gave evidence of his own special limitations
of knowledge and mental power and of his personal defects, as well
as of his powers. Each wrote upon a definite occasion, under special
historically grouped circumstances, from his own stand-point in the
progressively unfolded plan of redemption, and each made his own
special contribution to the fabric of God's word.

The divine agency, although originating in a different source, yet
emerges into the effect very much through the same channels. The
Scriptures have been generated, as the plan of redemption has been
evolved, through an historic process. From the beginning God has

dealt with man in the concrete, by self-manifestations and transactions. The revelation proceeds from facts to ideas, and has been gradually unfolded, as the preparation for the execution of the work of redemption has advanced through its successive stages. The general providence unfolding this plan has always been divine, yet has also been largely natural in its method while specially directed to its ends. . . . The Scriptures were generated through sixteen centuries of this divinely regulated concurrence of God and man, of the natural and the supernatural, of reason and revelation, of providence and grace. It is an organism consisting of many parts, each adjusted to all the rest, as the "many members" to the "one body." Each sacred writer was by God specially formed, endowed, educated, providentially conditioned, and then supplied with knowledge, naturally, supernaturally, or spiritually conveyed, so that he, and he alone could, and freely would, produce his allotted part. Thus God predetermined all the matter and form of the several books largely by the formation and training of the several authors, as the organist determines the character of his music as much when he builds his organ and when he tunes his pipes, as when he plays his keys. Each writer also is put providentially at the very point of view in the general progress of revelation to which his part assigns him. He inherits all the contributions of the past. He is brought into place and set to work at definite providential junctures, the occasion affording him object and motive, giving form to the writing God appoints him to execute.[5]

C. A. Briggs, *"Critical Theories of the Sacred Scriptures"* (1881)

[W]e are compelled to make the distinction between the doctrine of inspiration as stated by them [Hodge and Warfield], which is the doctrine of a large number of eminent theologians; and the church doctrine of inspiration as stated in the symbols.[6] . . . We

---

[5]A. A. Hodge and B. B. Warfield, "Inspiration," *The Presbyterian Review* 2 (April 1881): 229–230.
[6]By "symbols," Briggs means the key or central thoughts found in Scripture. Later in the article Briggs refers to "symbolical" inspiration, which is synonymous with his use of "plenary" inspiration.

hold . . . to *plenary* inspiration rather than verbal. It may be as the article states: "It [the term *plenary*] is in itself indefinite, and its use contributes nothing, either to the precision or the emphasis of the definition";[7] but this is as far as Scripture or the symbols of faith warrant us in going: it is as far as it is at all safe in the present juncture to advance in definition. *Verbal* inspiration is doubtless a more precise and emphatic definition, than *plenary* inspiration; but this very emphasis and precision imperil the doctrine of inspiration itself by bringing it into conflict with a vast array of objections along the whole line of Scripture and history, which must be met and overcome in incessant warfare, where both sides may count on doubtful victories, but where the weak, ignorant, and hesitating stumble and fall into divers temptations, and may make shipwreck of their faith. . . .

The Scriptures are lamps, vessels of the most holy character, but no less vessels of the divine grace than were the apostles and prophets who spake and wrote them. As vessels they have come into material contact with the forces of this world, with human weakness, ignorance, prejudice, and folly; their forms have been modified in the course of the generations, but their divine contents remain unchanged. We will never be able to attain the sacred writings as they gladdened the eyes of those who first saw them, and rejoiced the hearts of those who first heard them. If the external words of the original were inspired, it does not profit us. We are cut off from them forever. Interposed between us and them is the tradition of centuries and even millenniums. . . . Doubtless throughout the whole work of the authors "the Holy Spirit was present, causing his energies to flow into spontaneous exercises of the writers' faculties, elevating and directing where need be, and everywhere securing the errorless expression in language of the thought designed by God,"[8] but we cannot in the symbolical or historical use of the term call this providential care of his word or superintendence over its external production—inspiration. Such providential care and superinten-

---

[7]Hodge and Warfield, "Inspiration," 232.
[8]Ibid., 231.

dence is not different in kind with regard to the word of God, the visible church of God or the forms of the sacraments. Inspiration lies back of the external letter, it is that which gives the word its efficacy, it is the divine afflatus which enlightened and guided holy men to apprehend the truth of God in its appropriate forms; assured them of their possession of it, and called and enabled them to make it known to the church by voice and pen. This made their persons holy, their utterances holy, their writings holy, but only as the instruments, not as the holy thing itself. . . .

True criticism never disregards the letter, but reverently and tenderly handles every letter and syllable of the word of God, striving to purify it from all dross, brushing away the dust of tradition and guarding it from the ignorant and profane. But it is with no superstitious dread of magical virtue or virus in it, or anxious fears lest it should dissolve in their hands, but with an assured trust that it is the tabernacle of God, through whose external courts there is an approach to the Lord Jesus himself.[9]

In this next segment, B. F. Westcott, professor of divinity at Trinity College, University of Cambridge, affirms verbal and plenary inspiration, arguing that they are inseparably linked and perfectly display, as in the incarnation of the Christ, the "true antithesis" of human nature and divine agency.

B. F. Westcott, Introduction to the Study of the Gospels (1887)

On following out the lines of thought thus lightly sketched, it will appear, I think, that, from a Christian point of view, the notion of a perfect dynamical inspiration[10] is alone simple, sufficient, and natural. It presupposes that the same providential power which gave

---

[9]Source: C. A. Briggs, "Critical Theories of the Sacred Scriptures in Relation to their Inspiration," *The Presbyterian Review* 2 (July 1881): 551–552, 573–575.

[10]In his footnotes, Westcott admits that some may object to his term "dynamical inspiration" but confesses, "I can think of no better one which may be conveniently used to describe an influence acting upon living *powers*, and manifesting itself through them according to their natural laws, as distinguished from that influence which merely uses human *organs* for its outward expression, as, for instance, in the accounts of the demoniacs." Brooke Foss Westcott, *Introduction to the Study of the Gospels* (New York: Macmillan, 1882), 39.

the message selected the messenger; and implies that the traits of the individual character, and the peculiarities of manner and purpose, which are displayed in the composition and language of the sacred writings, are essential to the perfect exhibition of their meaning. It combines harmoniously the two terms in that relation of the finite to the infinite which is involved in the very idea of revelation. It preserves absolute truthfulness with perfect humanity, so that the nature of man is not neutralized, if we may thus speak, by the divine agency, and the truth of God is not impaired, but exactly expressed in one of its several aspects by the individual mind. Each element performs its perfect work; and in religion, as well as in philosophy, a glorious reality is based upon a true antithesis. The letter becomes as perfect as the spirit; and it may well seem that the image of the incarnation is reflected in the Christian Scriptures, which, I believe, exhibit the human and divine in the highest form, and in the most perfect union.[11]

DISTINGUISHING REVELATION AND INSPIRATION

As the debate in the late nineteenth century intensified over what constituted inspiration, conservative theologians saw the need for making clear distinctions between revelation and inspiration. One such theologian was Basil Manly, then professor of systematic theology at The Southern Baptist Theological Seminary. In 1888, he published a comprehensive work on the subject, *The Bible Doctrine of Inspiration*. The excerpt below from his book distinguishes the "two divine operations" and provides the reason why they must be understood separately.

Basil Manly, The Bible Doctrine of Inspiration: Explained and Vindicated (1888)

The supernatural interposition by which the Bible has been given to man implies two things, or consists of two divine operations, which, though usually concurring, are distinguished in their nature, viz.:

---

[11]Ibid., 41.

Revelation, which is that direct divine influence that imparts truth to the mind.

Inspiration, which is that divine influence that secures the accurate transference of truth into human language by a speaker or writer, so as to be communicated to other men.

These are not the same, not necessarily united, and ought not to be confounded. They have often been combined in the same person or writing. They must be combined, (as we think they are in the Bible,) in order to secure the infallible truth and divine authority we claim for it. But it is important to distinctness and accuracy of view to discriminate between them. To illustrate this distinction, we may refer,—

a. To those multitudes who heard Christ speak, and thus received a revelation, or to those who listened to the words uttered on Mount Sinai; for truth was presented to them in words by one who was God himself. But the hearers were not therefore inspired to record or relate these words upon divine authority. . . .

b. Many inspired men wrote under inspiration things which they knew without revelation, but their record or utterance of these things was divinely controlled. So when Luke . . . mentions the decrees for the enrollment of the Roman empire for taxation, or when John and Paul record what they themselves said or saw, we have no need to assume revelation as the source of their knowledge.

This distinction may enable us to see more clearly what the precise difference is between the strict and the lax views of inspiration among many who are really evangelical. Both agree that Christianity is true, notwithstanding all objections and difficulties. Both agree that revelation is supernatural, if given at all; and that it has been given; and this notwithstanding their confessed incapacity to understand or explain how it was given. But one class assume, or tend to assume, just at this point, that the writers were left to themselves mainly or altogether in recording what they knew. They allege a divine operation only in imparting to them knowledge on certain subjects; while the other class affirm a divine influence over the writers in their giving forth, as well as in receiving the truth. The former admit revelation freely, but are more or less uncertain or hesitating in affirming inspiration also. The latter affirm God's operation in both.[12]

DETERMINING INSPIRATION INDUCTIVELY

Rather than wholly dispensing with what was considered an outdated doctrine of inspiration, many scholars merged the old terminology with a higher-critical approach to the Bible. Robert F. Horton is a classic example of one such scholar. In this selection he proposes an inductive method for determining both the nature of inspiration and what can be considered inspired.

Robert F. Horton, Inspiration and the Bible (1889)

To find out what is the content of the term inspiration, we must set to work earnestly and diligently to find out what the Bible actually is. Instead of being hampered in all our inquiries by a foregone conclusion, and frightened from a candid investigation of fact by the fear lest the fact should shatter our theory of inspiration, we go to form our theory of inspiration from an examination of the facts. To use the language of logic, our inquiry becomes inductive instead of deductive; it is positive instead of metaphysical. The time, then, to formulate a doctrine of inspiration is when we have fairly and freely and fully investigated all that the inspired volume contains; only then can we draw together the varied phenomena and attempt to give an idea of the term not merely by example but by definition. We may, however, for clearness' and convenience' sake, adopt a formula at the outset which we hold subject to revision. We may express it thus. *We call our Bible inspired, by which we mean that by reading it and studying it we find our way to God, we find his will for us, and we find how we can conform ourselves to his will.*[13]

---

[12]Basil Manly, *The Bible Doctrine of Inspiration: Explained and Vindicated* (New York: A. C. Armstrong and Son, 1888), 36–38.

[13]Robert F. Horton, *Inspiration and the Bible* (London: T. Fisher Unwin, 1889), 12–13.

THE MEANING OF *THEOPNEUSTOS*

When B. B. Warfield wrote the entry on inspiration for James Orr's Bible encyclopedia in 1915, his position was neither new nor was his treatment of it exhaustive. But it was a clear and concise definition penned by a mature theologian who had already spent decades thinking, writing, and debating the particulars of the inspiration of Scripture. In the following portion Warfield defines what inspiration is—and what it is not—in light of the biblical expression found in 2 Timothy 3:16.

B. B. Warfield, "Inspiration" (1915)

The Greek term [*theopneustos*] has, however, nothing to say of *in*spiring or of *in*spiration: it speaks of only of a "spiring" or "spiration." What it says of Scripture is, not that it is "breathed into by God" or is the product of the divine "inbreathing" into its human authors, but that it is breathed out by God, "God-breathed," the product of the creative breath of God. In a word, what is declared by this fundamental passage is simply that the Scriptures are a divine product, without any indication of how God has operated in producing them. No term could have been chosen, however, which would have more emphatically asserted the divine production of Scripture than that which is here employed. The "breath of God" is in Scripture just the symbol of his almighty power, the bearer of his creative word. . . . When Paul declares, then, that "every Scripture," or "all Scripture," is the product of the divine breath, "is God-breathed," he asserts with as much energy as he could employ that Scripture is the product of a specifically divine operation.[14]

INTERNAL PROOFS FOR INSPIRATION

Conservative evangelical theologians approached the task of proving the inspiration of Scripture by gathering evidence from history,

---

[14]B. B. Warfield, "The Biblical Idea of Inspiration," *The Inspiration and Authority of the Bible*, ed. Samuel G. Craig (Phillipsburg, NJ: P&R, 1948), 133. Original: "Inspiration," *The International Standard Bible Encyclopedia*, 4 vols., ed. James Orr (Chicago: Howard-Severance, 1915), 3:1473–1483.

philosophy, and science (external) and by examining statements and implications in the Bible itself (internal). James M. Gray, the second president of Moody Bible Institute, contributed an article to *The Fundamentals*. The brief excerpt below follows Gray's summary of the external proofs for inspiration.

James M. Gray, "The Inspiration of the Bible—Definition, Extent and Proof" (c. 1910–1915)

But the strongest proof is the declarations of the Bible itself and the inferences to be drawn from them. Nor is this reasoning in a circle as some might think. In the case of a man as to whose veracity there is no doubt, no hesitancy is felt in accepting what he says about himself; and since the Bible is demonstrated to be true in its statements of fact by unassailable evidence, may we not accept its witness in its own behalf?

Take the argument from Jesus Christ as an illustration. He was content to be tested by the prophecies that went before on him, and the result of that ordeal was the establishment of his claims to be the Messiah beyond a peradventure. That complex system of prophecies, rendering collusion or counterfeit impossible, is the incontestable proof that he was what he claimed to be. But of course, he in whose birth, and life, and death, and resurrection such marvelous prophecies met their fulfillment, became, from the hour in which his claims were established, a witness to the divine authority and infallible truth of the sacred records in which these prophecies are found.

It is so with the Bible. The character of its contents, the unity of its parts, the fulfillment of its prophecies, the miracles wrought in its attestation, the effects it has accomplished in the lives of nations and of men, all these go to show that it is divine, and if so, that it may be believed in what it says about itself.[15]

---

[15] James M. Gray, "The Inspiration of the Bible—Definition, Extent and Proof," *The Fundamentals*, 4 vols., ed. R. A. Torrey et al. (1917; repr. Grand Rapids, MI: Baker, 2003), 2:19.

THE OLD BOOK IN A NEW WORLD

In the early decades of the twentieth century, the liberal or modern approach to the Bible in general and inspiration in particular continued to be widely embraced by mainstream Christianity. As its influence spread, the effects increasingly extended from the academy to the church. Pastors and laypeople who espoused the modern approach took confidence in their newfound liberty in Bible study and application and in the Christ who had been freed from the traditional confines of a literal Bible. In the first of the two following passages, Harry Emerson Fosdick presents a glowing appraisal of the benefits of modern thought on the inspiration of the Bible in the life of the Christian. The second passage by J. Gresham Machen strongly contests the liberal position and argues that the damage done to the doctrine of inspiration effectively shifts the authority of faith from the Bible to man.

Harry Emerson Fosdick, The Modern Use of the Bible (1924)

This leads us to our final statement about the consequences of the new approach to the Bible.[16] It restores to us the whole book. It gives to us a comprehensive, inclusive view of the Scriptures and enables us to see them, not piecemeal, but as a whole. Those of us who accept the modern knowledge of the Bible as assured and endeavor to put it to good use are continually being accused of tearing the book to pieces, of cutting out this or that, and of leaving a mere tattered patchwork of what was once a glorious unity. The fact is precisely the opposite. The new approach to the Bible once more integrates the Scriptures, saves us from our piecemeal treatment of them, and restores to us the whole book seen as a unified development from early and simple beginnings to a great conclusion. . . .

If someone protests that it [the new approach] spoils the idea of inspiration, I ask why. We used to think that God created the world by fiat on the instant, and then, learning that the world

---

[16]By "the new approach to the Bible," Fosdick means the various forms of "modern knowledge," i.e., study and exposition in light of higher criticism, new theories of inspiration expounded in the previous several decades, etc.

evolves, many were tempted to cry out that God did not create it at all. We now know that changing one's idea of a process does not in itself alter one's philosophy of origins. So we used to think of inspiration as a procedure which produced a book guaranteed in all its parts against error, and containing from beginning to end a unanimous system of truth. No well-instructed mind, I think, can hold that now. Our idea of the nature of the process has changed. What has actually happened is the production of a book which from lowly beginnings to great conclusions records the development of truth about God and his will, beyond all comparison the richest in spiritual issue that the world has known. Personally, I think that the Spirit of God was behind that process and in it. I do not believe that man ever found God when God was not seeking to be found. The under side of the process is man's discovery; the upper side of the process is God's revelation. Our ideas of the method of inspiration have changed; verbal dictation, inerrant manuscripts, uniformity of doctrine between 1000 B.C. and 70 A.D.—all such ideas have become incredible in the face of the facts. But one who earnestly believes in the divine Spirit will be led by the new approach to the Bible to repeat with freshened meaning and deepened content the opening words of the epistle to the Hebrews: "God, having of old times spoken unto the fathers in the prophets by divers portions and in divers manners, hath at the end of these days spoken unto us in his Son." . . .

Here, then, ends our study where any study of the Bible ought to bring us, standing in reverence before our Lord. For the message of the book is summed up in Christ. The book as a whole is best described as the record of the historical preparation for Christ, the earthly ministry of Christ, and the first impacts of Christ's personality and teaching on the lives of those who welcomed him. Nor have the modern uses of the Bible dimmed this fact. They rather have illuminated it. From them have come, not simply intellectual liberation from an old literalism, but incalculable spiritual enrichment as well through a quickened and clarified knowledge of Christ.

Let me bear a personal testimony as my closing word. From naive acceptance of the Bible as of equal credibility in all its parts because mechanically inerrant, I passed years ago to the shocking conviction that such traditional bibliolatry is false in fact and perilous in result. I saw with growing clearness that the Bible must be allowed to say in terms of the generations when its books were written what its words in their historic sense actually meant, and I saw that often this historic sense was not modern sense at all and never could be. There, like others, I have stood bewildered at the new and unaccustomed aspect of the book. But that valley of confusion soon passed. I saw that the new methods of study were giving far more than they were taking away. They have restored to us the historic Christ. They have led us to the abiding, reproducible experiences of the soul revealed through him. They have given us his imperishable Gospel freed from its entanglements, the Shekinah distinguished from the shrine, to be preached with a liberty, a reasonableness, an immediate application to our own age such as no generation of preachers in the church's history ever had the privilege of knowing before. Have no fear of the new truth! Let us fear only our own lack of wisdom, insight, courage, and spiritual power in using it for the redemption of the souls and societies of men.[17]

J. Gresham Machen, Christianity and Liberalism (1923)

This doctrine of "plenary inspiration" has been made the subject of persistent misrepresentation. Its opponents speak of it as though it involved a mechanical theory of the activity of the Holy Spirit. The Spirit, it is said, is represented in this doctrine as dictating the Bible to writers who were really little more than stenographers. But of course all such caricatures are without basis in fact, and it is rather surprising that intelligent men should be so blinded by prejudice about this matter as not even to examine for themselves the perfectly accessible treatises in which the doctrine of plenary inspiration is set forth. . . .

---

[17]Harry Emerson Fosdick, *The Modern Use of the Bible* (New York: Macmillan, 1924), 28–31, 272–273.

The modern liberal rejects not only the doctrine of plenary inspiration, but even such respect for the Bible as would be proper over against any ordinarily trustworthy book. But what is substituted for the Christian view of the Bible? What is the liberal view as to the seat of authority in religion?

The impression is sometimes produced that the modern liberal substitutes for the authority of the Bible the authority of Christ. He cannot accept, he says, what he regards as the perverse moral teachings of the Old Testament or the sophistical arguments of Paul. But he regards himself as being the true Christian because, rejecting the rest of the Bible, he depends upon Jesus alone. . . .

As a matter of fact, however, the modern liberal does not hold fast even to the authority of Jesus. Certainly he does not accept the words of Jesus as they are recorded in the Gospels. For among the recorded words of Jesus are to be found just those things which are most abhorrent to the modern liberal church, and in his recorded words Jesus also points forward to the fuller revelation which was afterwards to be given through his apostles. . . .

It is not true at all, then, that modern liberalism is based upon the authority of Jesus. It is obliged to reject a vast deal that is absolutely essential to Jesus's example and teaching—notably his consciousness of being the heavenly Messiah. The real authority, for liberalism, can only be "the Christian consciousness" or "Christian experience." But how shall the findings of the Christian consciousness be established? Surely not by a majority vote of the organized church. Such a method would obviously do away with all liberty of conscience. The only authority, then, can be individual experience; truth can only be that which "helps" the individual man. Such an authority is obviously no authority at all; for individual experience is endlessly diverse, and when once truth is regarded only as that which works at any particular time, it ceases to be truth. The result is an abysmal skepticism.

The Christian man, on the other hand, finds in the Bible the very word of God. Let it not be said that dependence upon a book is a dead or an artificial thing. The Reformation of the sixteenth century was founded upon the authority of the Bible, yet it set the world aflame. Dependence upon a word of man would be slavish, but dependence upon God's word is life. Dark and gloomy would be the world, if we were left to our own devices, and had no blessed word of God. The Bible, to the Christian is not a burdensome law, but the very Magna Charta of Christian liberty.

It is no wonder, then, that liberalism is totally different from Christianity, for the foundation is different. Christianity is founded upon the Bible. It bases upon the Bible both its thinking and its life. Liberalism on the other hand is founded upon the shifting emotions of sinful man.[18]

DIVINELY INSPIRED SCRIPTURE

From the earliest days of the modern debate, the majority of evangelical scholars denied that the means of communicating the inspired text was by divine dictation.[19] However, some evangelicals, in opposition to what they saw as an overemphasis on the humanity of the Bible, still espoused this view and considered the biblical writers mere penmen, composing only what God directly told them. In the excerpt below, W. A. Criswell, pastor of First Baptist Church in Dallas, author, and onetime president of the Southern Baptist Convention, defends his view of the divinity of Scripture.

W. A. Criswell, Why I Preach That the Bible Is Literally True (1969)

Who is the author of the Bible? Who spoke these words? Undoubtedly the author is God, and it is God who speaks these words. When we open the Scriptures, we find that sometimes the penman is Moses, sometimes it is David, sometimes it is Amos, or Hosea. When we turn further through the pages of the holy book, we see that sometimes the penman will be Matthew, Luke, John, or Paul. But did these men claim to be the authors of the Bible? Did

---

[18]J. Gresham Machen, *Christianity and Liberalism* (1923; Grand Rapids, MI: Eerdmans, repr. 1981), 73–74, 76.
[19]Hodge and Warfield strongly denounced the dictation theory in their essay "Inspiration."

they compose this tremendous volume? Do they divide the honors among themselves? No! For this volume is the writing of the living God. Each sentence was dictated by God's Holy Spirit. If Moses was employed to write, God guided the pen. If the prophet delivered a message to the people, it was God who formulated that message. If we find a description of the Lord Jesus Christ and a publication of his deeds and words, it will be according to the elective purpose and choice of the Holy Spirit. Everywhere in the Bible we find God speaking. It is God's voice, not man's. The words are God's words, the words of the eternal, invisible, Almighty Jehovah of heaven and earth.[20]

IN WHAT WAY IS THE BIBLE INSPIRED?

Evangelical theologians through the nineteenth and twentieth centuries have been charged by liberal and neo-orthodox scholars with giving such attention to the divine nature of Scripture that its human nature is nearly lost. While the segment from the article by A. A. Hodge and B. B. Warfield shows this was not in fact the case (at least for the Princeton theologians), the charge against the evangelical view of inspiration as a whole remained. In the first two excerpts below, neo-orthodox theologians Karl Barth and G. C. Berkouwer emphasize the humanness of Scripture and, in their own unique ways, how a book of human words becomes "inspired" with the holy word of God. In the final segment, Gordon Lewis, a member of the International Council on Biblical Inerrancy, contests the neo-orthodox position and argues the evangelical case.

Karl Barth, Church Dogmatics (1932–1968)

Of the book as we have it, we can only say: We recollect that we have heard in this book the word of God; we recollect, in and with the church, that the word of God has been heard in all this book and in all parts of it; therefore we expect that we shall hear the word of God in this book again, and hear it even in those places where

---

[20]W. A. Criswell, *Why I Preach That the Bible Is Literally True* (Nashville: Broadman, 1969), 68.

we ourselves have not heard it before. Yet the presence of the word of God itself, the real and present speaking and hearing of it, is not identical with the existence of the book as such. But in this presence something takes place in and with the book, for which the book as such does indeed give the possibility, but the reality of which cannot be anticipated or replaced by the existence of the book. A free divine decision is made. It then comes about that the Bible, the Bible *in concreto*, this or that biblical context . . . is taken and used as an instrument in the hand of God, i.e., it speaks to and is heard by us as the authentic witness to divine revelation and is therefore present as the word of God. . . . A genuine, fallible human word is at this centre the word of God: not in virtue of its own superiority, of its replacement by a word of God veiled as the word of man, still less of any kind of miraculous transformation, but, of course, in virtue of the privilege that here and now it is taken and used by God himself, like the water in the Pool of Bethesda. . . .

When we speak of the inspiration of the Bible or when we confess that the Bible is the word of God, on the one side, in the sphere of time and sense, in the concrete life of the church and of our own life as members of the church, we have to think of a twofold reality. There is first the question of the text of the biblical witness: or rather a definite portion of this text, which in a specific time and situation claims the attention of specific men or of a specific individual. If now it is true in time, as it is true in eternity, that the Bible is the word of God, then according to what we have just said, God himself now says what the text says. The work of God is done through this text. The miracle of God takes place in this text formed of human words. This text in all its humanity, including all the fallibility which belongs to it, is the object of this work and miracle. By the decision of God this text is now taken and used. And in the mystery of God it takes place that here and now this text acquires this determination. Yet it is still this text as such of which all this has to be said. It is as such that it will speak and attest, and be read and heard: and the word of God in it and through it, not alongside or behind it, not in some place which we have first to attain to or even create beyond the text. . . . Verbal inspiration does not mean the infallibility of the biblical word in its linguistic, historical and theological character as a human word. It means that the fallible and faulty human word is as such used by God and has to be received and heard in spite of its human fallibility.[21]

G. C. Berkouwer, Holy Scripture (1966)

The church has also confessed that Holy Scripture is the word of God against the background of this identity in prophecy and apostolate. The speaking of God through men is not a substitution of God's word for that of man. It remains man's own speech through the Holy Spirit in the mission to speak words (Jer. 26:5): the authorization of this human speech is found in this mission. Thus, in obedience to the word itself, the church speaks of Holy Scripture when reference is made to the books of the Bible, the gospel promised by the prophets in Holy Scripture (Rom. 1:2). The word "holy" does not imply a mysterious sacredness of a book, nor does it make human words into something divine. The confession concerning Scripture—with its emphatic "is"—does not imply the worship of a book. At issue is whether and in what way faith is related to the "gospel promised in Holy Scripture." Scripture is central because of its nature and intent. For this Scripture is only referred to because its sense and intent is the divine message of salvation. The words testify to it and all attention is drawn to it as the testimony "concerning his Son" (Rom. 1:3). Thus, they are "sacred writings" (2 Tim. 3:15) having their origin in the command of God (Rom. 16:26). Scripture is not severed from that which is real and truly human because of this "sacredness," but it comes to us in this human form. Of the humanly written (Scriptura) it is confessed: est Verbum Dei.[22]

[21]Karl Barth, Church Dogmatics, 5 vols., trans. G. T. Thomas and Harold Knight, ed. G. W. Bromiley and T. F. Torrance (Edinburgh: T&T Clark, 1956), 1(2):530, 532–533.
[22]G. C. Berkouwer, Holy Scripture, trans. Jack B. Rogers (Grand Rapids, MI: Eerdmans, 1975), 147–148.

Gordon R. Lewis, "The Human Authorship of
Inspired Scripture" (1980)

The Bible is not merely a compilation of human words written by people who were guided by the ordinary operations of the Holy Spirit, as are other books by believing, devout writers. These are not errant human words that merely function to lead people to Christ; they are words of conceptual truth that actually can lead people to the real Christ and faithfulness. The biblical concept of truth has two emphases—reliable information about reality and fidelity to it. One cannot substitute for the other. So also the biblical view of error has two emphases—mistaken information about what is or ought to be and unfaithfulness to this reality or morality. For an abundant Christian life a person must avoid both misinformation and unfaithfulness. . . .

Just as it is indispensable to eternal life to affirm that Jesus has come in human flesh, so it is crucial to evangelicalism to affirm that the written word has come in human words. It is not enough to say that the human words point to a word beyond all human expression. It is not enough to say that the time-bound human words witness to the timeless word. The confession of the early church was that Jesus is the Christ in true humanity. Analogously, the confession of the early church was that the Bible *is* God's word in all that it teaches. Many have pointed out that what the Bible says, God says; that what the prophet says, God says; that what the apostle says is God's commandment to the church. Just as relativism in ethics has changed "is good" to "is considered good by some in a given time or culture," so Berkouwer changes "God's word" to "a human witness to God's word." It sounds pious and humble and seems to resolve many critical questions, but the implications of that subtle change are as far-reaching as the nature and object of Christian faith, the nature of the message to be presented in missionary outreach, and the very substance of Christianity itself.[23]

---

[23]Gordon R. Lewis, "The Human Authorship of Inspired Scripture," *Inerrancy*, ed. Norman L. Geisler (Grand Rapids, MI: Zondervan, 1980), 259–260, 263–264.

3

[Inerrancy] is a ghost of modern evangelicalism to frighten children.

CHARLES AUGUSTUS BRIGGS

In 1961 Ralph H. Elliott, a professor at Midwestern Baptist Theological Seminary, one of five seminaries under the auspices of the Southern Baptist Convention, published a commentary on Genesis. As L. Russ Bush and Tom J. Nettles have it in their history of Baptists and the Bible, "Elliott's first sentence in *The Message of Genesis* begins to raise a question about the Mosaic authorship of the book."[1] That may be bad enough for some, but then Elliott's book took a more pernicious turn, questioning the historicity of the creation account and revealing throughout the book his dependence on critical method. In the aftermath, by the 1970s a full-fledged controversy raged through the Southern Baptist Convention, the largest Protestant denomination in the country, which is to say a controversy in the SBC will get national attention.

It became rather clear to theological conservatives in the SBC that there was a certain inability to deal with views like that of Elliott's circulating in the denomination due to the large number of moderates in key positions in the machinery that constitutes the

---

[1] L. Russ Bush and Tom J. Nettles, *Baptists and the Bible* (Nashville: Broadman & Holman, 1999), 327. See also Nancy Tatum Ammerman, *Baptist Battles: Social Change and Religious Conflict in the Southern Baptist Convention* (New Brunswick, NJ: Rutgers University Press, 1990).

SBC. By the end of the 1970s, Paige Patterson and Paul Pressler, a preacher and a judge respectively, became architects of a plan to take the denomination back to its conservative roots. They were very and speedily successful. By 1982, the more moderate or even liberal factions in the SBC were left scrambling, proposing an alternative venue to the national convention so they could develop some type of strategy of their own.

In 1983, the national meeting of the Southern Baptist Convention was held in Pittsburgh. The convention began as it typically did with a pastors' conference. As can be expected, the messages in that conference all circled around the authority, inspiration, and inerrancy of the Bible. One message in particular drove the point home. That previous fall, in the suburbs of Chicago, seven people had died from taking Tylenol pills, pills that had been tampered with and laced with potassium cyanide. That set off a national panic and was still quite fresh in the minds of Americans in the summer of 1983. One particular speaker at the pastors' conference held up a bottle of Tylenol. "If I knew there was one capsule in this bottle that was laced with cyanide, I would throw the whole bottle out," he thundered. Then he picked up his Bible. "If I knew of one error in this book"—everyone saw this coming—"I'd throw the whole thing out."[2] Inerrancy, in other words, either is or it isn't. And that was and continues to be the line of demarcation. The issue of inerrancy, since the 1890s, has been at the center of church trials, denominational controversies, and battles. Harold Lindsell didn't title his book *The Battle for the Bible* for no reason.[3]

Those more prone to peace than pugilism may question all of this controversy. The penchant for unity, for the body of Christ to be united in love, may legitimately give pause to celebrate this feature of twentieth-century American evangelicalism. And rightfully so. This story is not told to celebrate the fight. B. B. Warfield's words from Chapter 1 may serve well here. He reminds those squeamish

---

[2] I'm grateful to my dad, George Nichols, who attended the SBC pastors' conference that year and told me about that sermon.
[3] Harold Lindsell, *The Battle for the Bible* (Grand Rapids, MI: Zondervan, 1976).

about controversy that controversy rages only where convictions run strong. When it comes to the Bible's accuracy and reliability and truthfulness, convictions must run strong or the church could very easily and very quickly lose its way. To be sure, there are those who engage in controversy for controversy's sake, and there are those prone to abuse power and engage in political maneuvers under the guise of fighting for orthodoxy. But there are also those who have strong convictions. American evangelicals are known for taking the Bible seriously, for seeing in the Bible the true and reliable words of God. This chapter tells the story of those who held strong convictions, acted on those convictions, and helped make the Bible a crucial, central, and defining feature of American evangelicalism.

DENOMINATIONAL DISTURBANCES

To the Princetonians, inerrancy follows from inspiration, and a full and unmitigated inerrancy follows from verbal, plenary inspiration. Just as they had avoided a naive view of inspiration, however, they also avoided a naive view of inerrancy. Apparently, though, their view was not nuanced enough for Charles Augustus Briggs.

Briggs was a professor of Old Testament at Union Theological Seminary in New York, a seminary of the Presbyterian Church USA. Briggs was also ordained in the PCUSA. Briggs began to run afoul with his denomination in the early 1880s through articles he wrote for *The Presbyterian Review*, a journal he coedited with A. A. Hodge. Then came the publication of Briggs's inaugural address as the Edward Robinson Chair of Biblical Theology at Union, "The Authority of Holy Scripture," in 1891. The chair came about from a one hundred thousand dollar endowment—no small sum in 1891. This was a prominent position, perhaps one of the most prominent in theological seminaries in America. And from this platform, in his inaugural address, Briggs attacked verbal inspiration and inerrancy, all the while extolling the virtues of higher criticism. Briggs ventured, "Higher Criticism has rendered an inestimable service to this generation and to generations to come." Briggs went so far as to ask, "But on what authority do these theologians drive men from the Bible by this theory of inerrancy? The Bible itself nowhere makes this claim. The creeds of the church nowhere sanction it." Sensing that he was on a roll, Briggs crescendoed, "It is a ghost of modern evangelicalism to frighten children."[4]

That was enough for the denomination. The General Assembly of the PCUSA in 1891 did not uphold the appointment of Briggs to the Robinson chair, vetoing the decision of Union Seminary's board instead. In 1893, after the "Briggs case" made its way through his presbytery, the General Assembly suspended his ministerial credentials. All the while Union Seminary backed Briggs, and over him the seminary and the denomination severed ties. Briggs would be later ordained as an Episcopalian.

The Briggs case would prove to be a high-water mark in the debate over biblical inerrancy and higher criticism in America. Actually, it proved to be one of a series of high-water marks in this debate. Inerrancy would come to take its place as one of the so-called "fundamentals of the faith." The 1910 General Assembly of the PCUSA adopted the "Five Point Deliverance." This meant that ministerial candidates would have to affirm both the Westminster Standards and these five points, the first of which was the inspiration and inerrancy of Scripture, followed by Christ's virgin birth, Christ's atonement on the cross, Christ's bodily resurrection, and the belief in miracles. Some would round out these fundamentals by adding yet another point concerning Christ's second coming. By 1925, due to the ascendancy of moderate and liberal groups in the denomination, the "Five Point Deliverance" was dropped. In the early 1890s, Briggs represented the minority in the PCUSA. By 1925, the tables had turned.[5]

Similar controversy ran through the Northern Baptist Convention (now known as the American Baptist Churches in the USA, ABC-USA) in the 1920s. Various theological conservatives

---

[4]Charles Augustus Briggs, *Inaugural Address and Defense, 1891–1893* (New York: Arno Press, 1972), 33–35. The address was originally published by Charles Scribner's Sons in 1891.
[5]For the full story, see Bradley J. Longfield, *The Presbyterian Controversy: Fundamentalists, Modernists, and Moderates* (New York: Oxford University Press, 1991).

broke from the convention in the early years of the tumultuous 1920s, leaving the denomination in the hands of the moderates. William Bell Riley, who coined the term *fundamentalist*, emerged as one of the leaders of the conservatives. Prior to the 1920 Northern Baptist Convention meeting, fundamentalist leaders, Riley among them, gathered for a pre-meeting conference. Sermons on the inerrancy of the Bible and the evils of evolution reverberated throughout the Delaware Avenue Baptist Church in Buffalo, New York, the site of the conference. Riley himself ascended the pulpit to deliver a message. He argued that the question before the denomination could be boiled down to this: "Have we an inspired and infallible volume?" To Riley, inerrancy was one of three pillars of Baptist faith, the other two being the deity of Christ and the necessity of the new birth. Without inerrancy, he observed, "The first leg is gone from beneath the Baptist vase; and the denomination that was steady on its tripod will be found tottering on two remaining legs." The arguments of Riley and his compatriots fell upon deaf ears in the Northern Baptist Convention. By 1925, the more fiery fundamentalists abandoned the Northern Baptist Convention altogether.

Though coming a little late to all of this controversy, the Lutherans are not to be left out. The Lutheran Church-Missouri Synod is the most theologically conservative body of Lutheran churches in America. It has about half of the membership of the less conservative and largest body of Lutheran churches, the Evangelical Lutheran Church in America (ELCA), a denomination that came about as a merger of Lutheran groups, the two of significance being the Lutheran Church in America (LCA) and the American Lutheran Church (ALC), in 1988. One of the differences between the Missouri Synod Lutherans and these groups now known as the ELCA had to do with views of biblical authority, inerrancy, and higher criticism. But controversy over Scripture would strike home among Missouri Synod Lutherans. The controversy concerned the denomination's seminaries, both named Concordia, one being in St. Louis and one in Springfield, Illinois. The president of Concordia in

Springfield, Jacob A. Preus, surprisingly won election as president of the Missouri Synod in 1969 and began to put Concordia St. Louis, considered a haven for more liberal thought, under the microscope. By 1974 the president of Concordia St. Louis was suspended and a number of faculty members found suspect. In protest Concordia Seminary in Exile was established, with its name later changed to Christ Seminary-Seminex in the face of legal action. The issue, as with the Presbyterians and the Baptists, was the inerrancy of Scripture and higher criticism.

Inerrancy, it turns out, is an equal opportunity denominational offender. In addition to Presbyterian, Baptist, and Lutheran denominations, nineteenth-century battles over inerrancy also spilled into seminaries not denominationally affiliated and into parachurch organizations. Of these two categories, two cases stand out, that of Fuller Theological Seminary and the Robert Gundry case in the Evangelical Theological Society.

"NEW EVANGELICALISM"

Fuller Seminary was cofounded by and named for evangelist Charles E. Fuller. The other cofounder was the pastor of Park Street Church in Boston, Harold John Ockenga. From its beginnings in 1947, Fuller walked a tightrope of sorts between fundamentalism and the "new evangelicalism," a term coined by Ockenga. Fuller's early faculty consisted of Wilbur Smith, Carl Henry, and Harold Lindsell, among others. In the late 1950s and early 1960s, the controversy over inerrancy landed at Fuller, due in part to an influx of faculty not as committed to the doctrine. Among this group was Daniel Fuller, the son of the seminary's cofounder and namesake. Daniel Fuller had studied under G. C. Berkouwer at the Free University of Amsterdam. While Berkouwer began his career critical of Barth, he later migrated to a more appreciative stance of Barth and a critical stance of Warfield.[6] The younger Fuller followed suit. In an address to the Evangelical Theological Society's national meeting in 1967,

---

[6]See Carl W. Bogue, "Berkouwer and the Battle for the Bible," *Inerrancy and the Church*, ed. John Hannah (Chicago: Moody Press, 1984), 381–411.

Daniel Fuller posited two categories of Scripture: revelational Scripture, which is inerrant, and nonrevelational Scripture, which is not inerrant. Revelational Scripture concerns the plan of redemption and is error-free. Not so with the other parts of nonrevelational Scripture. Fuller's proposal was tantamount to limiting inerrancy. Or, to put it a bit more provocatively, Scripture contains errors.[7]

David Hubbard, president of Fuller for thirty years starting in 1963, also offered a corrective to Warfield and the doctrine of inerrancy. He claimed the word *inerrancy* was "too precise, too mathematical of a term to describe appropriately the way in which God's infallible revelation has come to us in a book."[8]

Historian George Marsden was intrigued by this story of Fuller, intrigued enough to write *Reforming Fundamentalism: Fuller Seminary and the New Evangelicalism* (1987). Marsden recounts conversations that Dan Fuller had with his parents, explaining to them that "Some of the chronologies in Scripture . . . are simply wrong." Marsden also recounts Dan Fuller's battles with faculty members from Gleason Archer to E. J. Carnell over Dan's desire to change Fuller's creed. Eventually Dan Fuller was appointed dean of the seminary, and David Hubbard, as mentioned, was appointed to the presidency. Though Hubbard and Dan Fuller were not exactly on the same page when it came to their respective revisionist views of inerrancy, they differed with the likes of Harold Lindsell, then vice president of the seminary, Wilbur Smith, and Gleason Archer. All three exited Fuller. Lindsell was off to *Christianity Today*, with Smith and Archer landing at Trinity Evangelical Divinity School. To be sure there were politics and personalities involved in all of this, but in the end this turmoil at Fuller came down to inerrancy.[9]

And then there is the case of Robert Gundry's expulsion from the Evangelical Theological Society (ETS). Founded in 1949, ETS had but a singular doctrinal statement: "The Bible alone, and the

[7]Daniel P. Fuller, "Benjamin B. Warfield's View of Faith and History," *Bulletin of the Evangelical Theological Society* 11:2 (Spring 1968), 80.
[8]David Allen Hubbard, *Fuller Theological Seminary Bulletin* 18:1 (March 1968).
[9]George M. Marsden, *Reforming Fundamentalism: Fuller Seminary and the New Evangelicalism* (Grand Rapids, MI: Eerdmans, 1987), 201.

Bible in its entirety, is the Word of God written and is therefore inerrant in the autographs." In the past few years, the society added a statement on the Trinity. It was this singular statement on inerrancy, though, that led to the ouster of Robert Gundry. In 1982 Gundry published *Matthew: A Commentary on His Literary and Theological Art*, in which he argued, following redaction criticism, that Matthew crafted his telling of the life of Christ, especially using ahistorical literature in his telling of the birth narrative. Gundry was brought up on charges in a motion presented to the society by Roger Nicole. He was initially exonerated, but only initially. Gundry, it turns out, had poor timing. Norman Geisler, a prominent figure in the defense of inerrancy, would not sit idly by, and at the time Geisler was prominent in the International Council on Biblical Inerrancy. Geisler engineered a full-court press to have the motion to ask Gundry to resign voted on at the 1983 meeting of the society. The vote was taken, and the motion carried. Gundry resigned.[10]

The case of Fuller Seminary in the late 1960s and 1970s and the case of Robert Gundry in the early 1980s, as well as the denominational battles mentioned earlier, reveal how deeply controversial the subject of inerrancy was. To stem the drift away from inerrancy and to shore up those who held it, the International Council on Biblical Inerrancy was formed in 1978, holding its first major conference or summit in Chicago in the last days of October of that year.

THE CHICAGO STATEMENT

At that first major conference, the attendees, numbering over three hundred and including evangelical leaders from a variety of denominations and theological persuasions, signed off on the Chicago Statement. Some of the figures involved in this statement include Carl F. H. Henry, James M. Boice, J. I. Packer, John MacArthur (Sr. and Jr.), Francis Schaeffer, Paige Patterson, Robert D. Preus, and W. A. Criswell. The statement starts with five short statements

---

[10]For the full story, see "Evangelical Scholars Remove Robert Gundry for His Views on Matthew," *Christianity Today*, February 3, 1984.

regarding Scripture's divine origin, verbal and plenary inspiration, and full and unmitigated inerrancy. Then the statement offers nineteen articles of affirmations and denials, explicitly laying out what the ICBI is saying (affirmations) and what it is not saying (denials) about the doctrine of Scripture. The first five articles concern revelation, while the next five concern inspiration. The last nine articles address inerrancy.[11]

The signatories to ICBI, as mentioned, represented a variety of denominations. They also represented a variety of circumstances and contexts. Some were pastors who signed on because they viewed the doctrine of inerrancy as crucial to preaching. W. A. Criswell stands out among this group. In his book *Why I Preach That the Bible Is Literally True* he says, "Let me speak directly to Southern Baptists. If our preachers, evangelists, pastors, churches, and institutions are true to that expression of faith [of inerrancy], we shall live. If we repudiate it, we shall die."[12] Also included among this group of signatories is fellow Southern Baptist Paige Patterson, right in the throes of engineering the conservative takeover (or reclamation) of his denomination. Robert Preus joined in fresh from the battles in the Lutheran Church-Missouri Synod. Theologians and pastors not so fresh from battle also joined in, knowing that it is just as crucial to maintain the view of inerrancy as it is to fight for it.

What is further remarkable about the list of signatories is how much and how deeply they disagreed with each other on all sorts of doctrinal matters. But on this one issue of inerrancy, they were able to come together. It is true that the twentieth century was a century of battles for the Bible over the doctrine of inerrancy. It is equally true, and this fact is often overlooked in the telling of the story, that the twentieth century was also a century of remarkable unity among American evangelicals over the doctrine of inerrancy. The unity is remarkable because American evangelicals seem to so enjoy

---

[11]The Chicago Statement may be found in Norman L. Geisler, ed., *Inerrancy* (Grand Rapids, MI: Zondervan, 1979). This book contains not only the statement but also fourteen essays, originally delivered as lectures at the 1978 ICBI Chicago Summit.
[12]W. A. Criswell, *Why I Preach That the Bible Is Literally True* (Nashville: Broadman Press, 1969), 159.

disagreeing with each other. Scripture, and specifically inerrancy, did divide, but it also united.

One divide that was mostly left intact despite all this unity concerned the African-American church. Debates over inerrancy simply didn't run that deeply within the African-American church. For one thing, in the 1900s, and especially in the 1960s and 1970s, the African-American church had other pressing issues to contend with, namely segregation, race-based oppression, and the civil rights movement. Secondly, and this is rather telling, the African-American church tended rather reflexively to acknowledge and therefore submit to the Bible as the word of God. The debates over inerrancy largely played out in white American Christianity. It's not that the African-American church took inerrancy lightly. On the contrary, African-American Christianity had such a firm sense of biblical authority that the challenges to inerrancy that flourished in many places on the American church landscape never even gained a hearing.

Chris Rice relays the story of Spencer Perkins, the son of John Perkins, being interviewed for Voice of Calvary Church's elder board. Spencer was asked to give his position on the inspiration and authority of Scripture. He replied, "Black people take it for granted that the Bible's from God, and we don't require a sophisticated explanation."[13] Such commendable faith and humility were often lacking in the predominantly white American churches toward the Bible. And in many of those churches, the Bible was not taken reflexively as the word of God that stands over us and requires submission. In fact, sophisticated arguments were offered to diminish the Bible's authority. Consequently, sophisticated defenses were required. Such a defense was the Chicago Statement on Inerrancy.

The first of these articles of the Chicago Statement to address inerrancy specifically, Article XI, asserts that Scripture is infallible and inerrant. Since these words are generally regarded as synonymous, the fact that the Chicago Statement addresses it warrants some

---

[13]Spencer Perkins, quoted in Chris Rice, *Grace Matters: A True Story of Race, Friendship, and Faith in the Heart of the South* (San Francisco: Jossey-Bass, 2002), 40.

explanation. Those uncomfortable with inerrancy preferred the term *infallible*, which was interpreted by some as nothing more than a sidestep maneuver or semantic tactics. The Chicago Statement, however, wished to be clear on the matter. The next article further clarifies matters. Article XII affirms that Scripture is "free from all falsehood, fraud, or deceit," denying that "Biblical infallibility and inerrancy are limited to spiritual, religious, or redemptive themes, exclusive of assertions in the fields of history and science." This point addressed specifically arguments like that of Daniel Fuller, who it may be recalled posited a distinction between revelational Scripture and nonrevelational Scripture.

The Chicago Statement was nuanced enough to acknowledge that inerrancy is not negated by "Biblical phenomena such as a lack of modern technical precision, irregularities of grammar or spelling, observational descriptions of nature, the reporting of falsehoods, the use of hyperbole and round numbers, the topical arrangement of material, variant selections of material in parallel accounts, or the use of free citations." These items were precisely the issue regarding challenges to inerrancy. Opponents of inerrancy, in other words, used the issues mentioned here to show that inerrancy is a wrongheaded concept. Like the Princetonians, who attempted to avoid a naive stance on inspiration, ICBI attempts to avoid a naive inerrancy. The reader of Scripture may be confronted with challenges, but those challenges do not rise to the level of negating inerrancy, the Chicago Statement maintains. Thinking back to the case of Fuller Seminary, Marsden recalls a heated discussion in a faculty meeting over discrepancies in the Bible. In an exchange between Edward Carnell and Dan Fuller, Carnell turned to Fuller to say, "My list of discrepancies is longer than yours, Dan Fuller." Carnell had little appreciation for Dan Fuller's assumption that only he was confronting Scripture's problems. To hear the rest of the story, as Marsden tells it, is instructive, "[b]ut that [long list of discrepancies] did not matter, because if we come to the Bible as the verbally inspired word of

God we find that we have fewer problems with our system than with any competing system," Dan Fuller's limited inerrancy system included.[14]

Figure 3.1
Inerrancy Timeline

1893	Warfield publishes "The Inerrancy of the Original Autographs."
1910	PCUSA General Assembly adopts the "Five Point Deliverance."
1910–1915	*The Fundamentals* are published in twelve volumes, edited by R. A. Torrey, A. C. Dixon, and others.
1925	PCUSA drops "Five Point Deliverance."
1946	Ned B. Stonehouse and Paul Woolley edit and publish *The Infallible Word* by Westminster Seminary faculty.
1947	Fuller Seminary is founded.
1949	Evangelical Theological Society (ETS) is founded.
1957	E. J. Young publishes *Thy Word Is Truth*.
1961	Ralph H. Elliott publishes *The Message of Genesis*.
1962	Fuller Seminary changes statement of faith on inerrancy.
1973	"Ligonier Statement" on inerrancy is signed and published.
1976	Harold Lindsell publishes *The Battle for the Bible*.
1977	International Council on Biblical Inerrancy is formed.
1978	ICBI members sign "The Chicago Statement on Biblical Inerrancy."
1979	Jack B. Rogers and Donald K. McKim publish *The Authority and Interpretation of the Bible*.
1980	Norman L. Geisler edits and publishes *Inerrancy* by ICBI members.
1982	Robert L. Gundry publishes *Matthew* commentary.
1983	Gundry resigns ETS membership.
1984	John Hannah edits and publishes *Inerrancy and the Church* by ICBI members.
1984	John Warwick Montgomery edits and publishes *God's Inerrant Word* by ICBI members.
1984	Gordon Lewis and Bruce Demarest edit and publish *Challenges to Inerrancy* by ICBI members.
1987	ICBI disbands.
1988	Harvie Conn edits and publishes *Inerrancy and Hermeneutic* by Westminster Seminary faculty.

INERRANCY, SCRIPTURE, AND CHURCH HISTORY (OR, CAN SO MANY BE SO WRONG?)

The final articles of the Chicago Statement connect inerrancy first with Scripture, claiming that "inerrancy is grounded in the teaching of the Bible about inspiration" (Article XV), and then with church history, stating that "the doctrine of inerrancy has been integral to

---

[14]Edward J. Carnell, cited in Marsden, *Reforming Fundamentalism*, 213.

the church's faith throughout history" (Article XVI). These two points, the biblical teaching on inerrancy and the affirmation of inerrancy in church history, have been contested items ever since the days of Charles Augustus Briggs. It may be recalled that Briggs flat-out denied that the Bible teaches inerrancy and posited the absence of inerrancy in the annals of church history. Briggs certainly wasn't the only one to make such claims. Since his days these challenges to inerrancy have been repeated again and again.

When it comes to Scripture, defenders of inerrancy tend to start with Christ's use of the Old Testament. On this score, John Murray concluded, "The inescapable fact is that the mass of direct and indirect statements leads to one conclusion that, for our Lord, the Scripture, just because it was *Scripture*, just because it fell within the denotation of the formula, 'it is written,' was a finality. [Christ's] attitude is one of meticulous acceptance and reverence." Murray adds, "The only explanation of such an attitude is that what Scripture said, God said." After Christ's use of Scripture, defenders of inerrancy look to various biblical texts that speak of the purity (Ps. 12:6) and the truthfulness of God's word (Num. 23:19; Prov. 30:5; Matt. 24:35), or they point out the numerous references to God as a speaker of truth, not a teller of lies (2 Sam. 7:28; Heb. 6:18). Not to mention Paul. Paul knew his Old Testament, the very same Old Testament that is claimed to be rife with errors in genealogical records or historical detail. Yet, it was essentially the Old Testament that Paul was referring to when he claimed that "All Scripture is breathed out [inspired] by God" (2 Tim. 3:16). To posit that Scripture contains error is to posit that God lies.

Others point to 1 Peter 1:24–25 as evidence of the fully truthful and inerrant nature of Scripture:

> All flesh is like grass
> and all its glory like the flower of the grass.
> The grass withers,
> and the flower falls,
> but the word of the Lord remains forever.

This text echoes words of Christ from Matthew 5:18: "For truly, I say to you, until heaven and earth pass away, not an iota, not a dot, will pass from the Law until all is accomplished." E. J. Young offers a concluding point to the biblical data: "The Bible, according to its own claims, is breathed from God. To maintain that there are flaws or errors in it is the same as declaring that there are flaws or errors in God himself."[15]

Not all are convinced by these and other such texts. James Barr counters, "There is no 'the Bible' that 'claims' to be divinely inspired, there is no 'it' that has a 'view of itself.'"[16] Barr's point, which has been made by others, is that these texts are only talking about individual texts, not offering blanket statements about the whole Bible. Others have pointed out, however, that Barr misses the preponderance of the evidence. It's not as if there are only a few scattered texts that lay claim to Scripture's truthfulness. Many such texts overflow the pages of Scripture. The preponderance of references is striking and telling.

Then there is church history. Opponents of inerrancy insist that verbal, plenary inspiration and the correlate of inerrancy are a creation of Warfield and the Princetonians, not present in church history. Two areas of focus tend to come into view, the early church fathers and the Reformers.

Historians use the term *anachronism*, a helpful term that may need some defining. It literally means "across time." But when historians use it, they often mean a bit more, and they tend to use it in a negative light. In this negative use, being anachronistic means applying the standards or particular understandings or even vocabulary of a later age or time to a previous age or time. Doctrines tend to get developed over time, with successive generations clarifying terms and summarizing data. Most times this occurs in the face of direct challenge to biblical teaching. That is clearly the case in the doctrine of Scripture. In light of the challenges brought on by the modern age, the Princetonians did offer new terms to describe what

---

[15]E. J. Young, *Thy Word Is Truth* (Grand Rapids, MI: Eerdmans, 1957), 123.
[16]James Barr, *Fundamentalism* (London: SCM, 1977), 78.

had constituted orthodox belief in the church about the Bible. Those new terms were *verbal, plenary inspiration* and *inerrancy*. It might have been enough for previous generations in the church simply to say that Scripture is true or even wholly true. But in the modern age, one is forced to add to that, claiming that Scripture is wholly and fully true in all that it affirms in matters pertaining to faith and in matters pertaining to science and history. The upshot of this is to say that it shouldn't surprise us that the church fathers or the Reformers don't talk about Scripture in the same way that the Princetonians, and those since them, do. It would be wrong to conclude, however, that because identical language is not used, therefore the church fathers and the Reformers on the one hand think differently about Scripture than do the Princetonians and those who follow suit with them on the other hand.

This is a significant charge against the inerrancy position and warrants a restatement. Critics of the inerrancy position charge that the Princetonians and those since them who have held to verbal, plenary inspiration and inerrancy are anachronistic in that those of the Princetonian position force others who preceded them into their camp. When a church father speaks of the Bible as fully truthful, to make this concrete, the Princetonians claim them on their side. Critics charge that this is illegitimate, that it reads too much into these fathers. There is a twofold irony here. First, looking for the same exact words is wrongheaded. One should be looking for the same concepts in these historical figures. The historical record reveals those same concepts given expression by the Princetonians to be present in the early church and Reformers, as seen below. The second part of the irony is that the charge of anachronism lands not at the feet of the Princetonians but at the feet of the critics who take those who speak freely and deeply about the full truthfulness of Scripture to be all the while harboring positions of limited inerrancy. That conclusion simply does not make sense.

What we do find when we peer into church history, starting with the church fathers, is a long list of citations resting on the complete truthfulness and trustworthiness of Scripture. Clement of Rome, writing in 96, exhorted, "Look carefully into the Scriptures, which are the true utterances of the Holy Spirit." Another Clement, Bishop of Alexandria, declared similarly, "I could produce ten thousand Scriptures of which not 'one tittle will pass away' without being fulfilled. For the mouth of the Lord, the Holy Spirit, has spoken these things." As for a statement about the whole Bible, Origen once observed, "For the proof of our statements, we take testimonies from that which is called the Old Testament and that which is called the New—which we believe to be divine writings." In addition, much of the writings of the church fathers was apologetic in nature as they engaged the views of false teachers both within and without the church. These apologists, such as Justin Martyr or Athenagoras, often contrasted the "false teachings" with the "true teachings" of Scripture.

At the ICBI summit in 1978, Robert D. Preus, coming from the battle for the Bible among the Missouri Synod Lutherans, read a paper on "The View of the Bible Held by the Church: The Early Church Through Luther," later published in the volume *Inerrancy*, edited by Norman Geisler. In that essay, Preus offers this conclusion in the first sentence: "That the Bible is the Word of God, inerrant and of supreme divine authority, was a conviction held by all Christians and Christian teachers through the first 1,700 years of church history."[17] Such blanket statements tend to get historians in trouble. But with a bit of qualifying, Preus's statement rings true.

Also at the ICBI Summit, John Gerstner delivered a paper on "The View of the Bible Held by the Church: Calvin and the Westminster Divines," which was also published in the volume *Inerrancy*, edited by Geisler. Gerstner lists the ways Calvin refers to Scripture, all of these being direct quotes from Calvin: "the sure and infallible record," "the inerring standard," "the pure Word of God," "the infallible rule of His Holy Truth," "free from every stain

---

[17]Robert D. Preus, "The View of the Bible Held by the Church: The Early Church Through Luther," in *Inerrancy*, ed. Norman Geisler (Grand Rapids, MI: Zondervan, 1979), 357.

or defect," "the inerring certainty," "the certain and unerring rule," "unerring light," "infallible Word of God," "has nothing belonging to man mixed with it," "inviolable," "infallible oracles."[18] A later book of essays under the auspices of the ICBI expanded this discussion of inerrancy in church history. With John Hannah serving as editor, *Inerrancy and the Church* seeks to advance a singular thesis: "The thesis of this book is that the position of the church, as it has been delineated by scholars, clerics, and teachers, is that of the absolute authority and inerrancy of the Scriptures. That was the view of Augustine, Luther, and Calvin, as well as of the entire church; inerrancy is the 'central church tradition.'"[19] The inclusion of those three figures in particular was intentional. Those three are presented by Jack Rogers and Donald McKim as specifically not affirming inerrancy, as part of the Rogers/McKim proposal that inerrancy is a creation of the Princetonians.

Garnering quotes from historical figures can be a tricky business. But, just as with the quotes from Scripture, the various quotes from figures in church history must be seen in their preponderance. These data that point to figures from church history espousing a view of Scripture akin to inerrancy are not few and scattered but many and prominent. Edith Blumhofer, a historian at Wheaton, once jokingly quipped that historians, if you pay them enough money and tell them what view you want supported, will find you a quote. There is some truth embedded in the humor. You can find quotes to support just about any position. The discerning reader will be looking, however, at the full weight of the evidence. As with Scripture's self-claims, claims from church history to a view of Scripture that accords with verbal, plenary inspiration and inerrancy are not found lacking but are found in abundance. It is telling that Rogers and McKim never published a formal response to the work of the ICBI regarding these historical arguments.

---

[18] John Gerstner, "The View of the Bible Held by the Church: Calvin and the Westminster Divines," in *Inerrancy*, 391.
[19] John D. Hannah, ed., *Inerrancy and the Church* (Chicago: Moody Press, 1984), ix.

INERRANCY AS AN EXISTENTIAL PROBLEM

Until now, this discussion has mainly concerned inerrancy as an academic debate. Most evangelicals living in the twenty-first century, however, live unaware of the goings on in Fuller Seminary's faculty meetings, ETS meetings, debates over the views of Scripture held by the church fathers, and debates over Karl Barth. But evangelicals do read Scripture, and sometimes they have questions, bordering on doubts, about what they are reading. E. J. Young framed it this way: "There are good Christian people who would like to believe in the absolute trustworthiness of the Bible, yet who hesitate because they are convinced that there are mistakes in the Bible." Young continues, "In serious Bible study one often encounters difficulties, and the solution to these difficulties is not always apparent."[20]

Other concerns may arise from those who think through the issue of the autograph copies of Scripture versus manuscripts and translations or versions of Scripture. The Chicago Statement, and just about every other statement on inerrancy, restricts inspiration and inerrancy to the original autographs, the term *autograph* referring to the original copy of the biblical book penned by the biblical author. The simple truth is, we no longer have the autographs. Instead, we have manuscripts, copies of the text. But most people are unable to read the Bible in the original languages and cannot read through these manuscripts, which means that they are dependent on translations and versions—yet another step (many steps actually—but that's another story) removed from the original autograph. So now the dilemma can be stated: one cannot hold up a translation of the Bible (even if it is the ESV) and say, "This is 100 percent the word of God, inspired and inerrant." That was very well true of the original autographs, but it simply doesn't apply to our English or any other translations of the Bible.

In our pluralistic environment, there also is the challenge of the Bible's claiming to be the true word of God alongside the claims of other religions about their religious texts. Is it simply cultural impe-

---

[20]Young, *Thy Word Is Truth*, 165.

rialism that leads one to say that the Bible, the book of what developed into a distinctively western religion of Christianity, is true?

In light of these challenges, the doctrine of inerrancy can be viewed two ways. The first is as an embarrassment at worst or simply unhelpful at best. It is curious that recent developments among evangelicals have expressed uneasiness with the term *inerrancy*. Andrew McGowan has recently claimed that the term *inerrancy* simply isn't helpful. And Kenton L. Sparks has argued that the view of inerrancy is a barrier for evangelical biblical scholars seeking to engage in serious biblical scholarship. As with developments in inspiration, we are simply too close to these developments to ascertain their full impact on evangelicalism and on the doctrine of Scripture. They do represent something that has been brewing ever since those heated discussions in the Fuller faculty meetings, a growing uneasiness by self-proclaimed evangelicals with the Princetonian and Chicago Statement formulations of inerrancy.[21]

The second way we can respond to the challenges facing inerrancy takes us in a different direction—humble acceptance of the trustworthiness of God's word, somewhat akin to the humble acceptance of God himself. God and his ways are sometimes troubling (if we're honest). Apparent difficulties abound (if we're honest). Yet a life of faith means trusting in God. This is no mere foolish acceptance. We can still question and think and seek resolution. So it could possibly be with God's word. E. J. Young put it this way: "When therefore we meet difficulties in the Bible let us reserve judgment. If any explanation is not at hand, let us freely acknowledge that we do not know all things, that we do not know the solution. Rather than hastily proclaim the presence of error is it not the part of wisdom to acknowledge our ignorance?"[22]

Again, this approach does not mean foolish acceptance, and it does not mean that evangelical biblical scholars are cut off from

---

[21]A. T. B. McGowan, *The Divine Authenticity of Scripture: Retrieving an Evangelical Heritage* (Downers Grove, IL: IVP Academic, 2008); Kenton Sparks, *God's Word in Human Words: An Evangelical Appropriation of Critical Biblical Scholarship* (Grand Rapids, MI: Baker Academic, 2008), 256, 373–374.

[22]Young, *Thy Word Is Truth*, 185.

engaging in serious biblical scholarship or from engaging in the work of critical biblical scholars. It does mean, though, humbly accepting that we may not have all of the answers to all of the questions raised in reading the Bible or in thinking about the place of the Bible in our current cultural place and time. The doctrine of inspiration forces those who live in the modern world to look beyond themselves in their quest to understand the world—something moderns do not always reflexively or willingly do. The doctrine of inerrancy also requires something of those living in the modern and now postmodern world.

INERRANCY AND INCARNATION

A contemporary controversy over inspiration and inerrancy is occurring at Westminster Theological Seminary. This controversy centers on Peter Enns, an Old Testament professor, and his book *Inspiration and Incarnation.* Enns argues that the incarnational analogy can help clear up some of the issues related to the doctrine of inspiration and biblical criticism. Enns argues that the human side of inspiration doesn't always receive its due in evangelical formulations of the doctrine of Scripture and in evangelical biblical scholarship. The specific issue at Westminster is whether or not Enns's views square with the Westminster Standards, the doctrinal statement for Westminster Seminary. That debate will likely be a rather divided issue and will continue on for some time. The turn to the incarnation, though, precedes Enns's book.[23]

In a very different way from Peter Enns, Karl Barth also focused on the incarnation for his model of understanding inspiration and the question of inerrancy. Karl Barth argued that the evangelical doctrine of inspiration and inerrancy is akin to docetic views of the incarnation. Docetism (from the Greek word *dokeo*, meaning "to appear") is a heresy from the days of the early church that held that Christ only appeared to be human, that Christ wasn't fully human. This view was so zealous for the divinity of Christ that it could not

---

[23]Peter E. Enns, *Inspiration and Incarnation: Evangelicals and the Problem of the Old Testament* (Grand Rapids, MI: Baker Academic, 2005).

allow for Christ's humanity. The view was also overly influenced by Plato and his ambivalence toward matter and material existence. When the claim is made that certain views of inspiration are docetic, the meaning is that they pay lip service to the human side of the composing of Scripture and don't take it seriously. The divine constantly overrides the human so that one essentially has a divine book, not a divine-human book. Karl Barth, G. C. Berkouwer, and Paul King Jewett (of Fuller Seminary) all made this claim against the reigning evangelical view of inspiration and inerrancy.

Charles C. Ryrie made an observation that bears repeating: "But if it were true (which it is not) that those who hold to the total inerrancy of the Bible are espousing a heresy akin to Docetism, then it would be equally true that those who hold to any kind of errancy support a doctrine analogous to Ebionitism."[24] The Ebionite heresy is another heresy from the early church concerning Christ. This group denied Christ's deity. What Ryrie is doing is turning the tables on Barth, Berkouwer, and Jewett. Ryrie further counters that the orthodox formulation of the incarnation holds that Christ is the God-man, full humanity and full divinity united in the one person of Christ in such a way that Christ is perfectly sinless. So the orthodox doctrine of Scripture, Ryrie argues, is such that the word of God is both fully divine and fully human in such a way that it is perfectly without error.

Gordon Lewis also addressed this issue of the incarnational analogy, admitting that at times the human side of Scripture is unfortunately downplayed by those holding to inerrancy, countering, "Just as it is indispensable to eternal life to affirm that Jesus has come in human flesh, so it is crucial to evangelicalism to affirm that the written Word has come in human words." But then Lewis adds, "It is not enough to say that the human words point to a Word beyond all human expression. . . . The Bible is God's Word in all that it teaches." Lewis here is directly responding to Barth and Berkouwer's claim that the words of the Bible are a human witness to the word of God. Lewis continues, "It sounds pious and humble

---

[24]Charles C. Ryrie, *What You Should Know about Inerrancy* (Chicago: Moody Press, 1981), 53.

and seems to resolve many critical questions" to shift from *the Bible is God's word* to *the Bible is a human witness to God's word*, "but the implications of that subtle change are as far-reaching as the nature and object of the Christian faith, the nature of the message to be presented in missionary outreach, and the very substance of Christianity itself."[25] Christ is not merely a witness to God; Christ, as the God-man, is God. So too Scripture is not merely a witness to the word of God; Scripture, as the divine-human book of revelation, is the word of God.

CONCLUSION

In their discussions on the incarnation and doctrines of inspiration and inerrancy, Charles Ryrie and Gordon Lewis draw from the original formulation of the doctrines by the Princetonians. Warfield's notion of concursus stressed the full contribution of both the divine and human in the composition of Scripture in such a way that neither diminished the other. Warfield applied the notion of concursus to the incarnation and even to the life of faith, the interaction between the divine and the human in the course of life. Concursus for Warfield entailed mystery. Warfield couldn't always ferret out the mystery, but he was always humbled by it, holding to it without flinching or wavering.

The doctrine of inerrancy has been a challenging doctrine for evangelicals in the twentieth century. It was a line of demarcation for decades between fundamentalists and liberals. It divided denominations and disrupted seminaries. The doctrine became a source of contention within evangelicalism as well. If these early years of the twenty-first century are any indicator, it seems that it remains a challenge today. But, as noted, the doctrine also became a unifying point for evangelicals. Imagine locking three hundred evangelicals in a room and having them come up with something upon which they agree. Further imagine that what they agree upon is a document of no fewer than nineteen articles. It might be inappropriate

---

[25]Gordon Lewis, "The Human Authorship of Inspired Scripture," in *Inerrancy*, ed. Geisler, 263–264.

to refer to what happened at the first summit of the International Council on Biblical Inerrancy as a miracle, but it does seem to come close. Evangelicals have famously held to a high view of Scripture. For a moment three hundred of them, as well as the constituencies they represented, agreed on the inerrancy of Scripture. Doctrine sometimes divides, to be sure, but sometimes, when the stakes are high, it can also gloriously unite.

The horizon may contain more battles, however, more occasions for disunity. Hopefully, in the throes of all these battles for the Bible, the church, from the halls of the academy to the pulpit and the pew, will be deepened in its commitment to hear and obey the word of God that cannot be broken.

4

The controversy over the inerrancy of Scripture in the modern age in many ways followed on the heels of the inspiration debate, raging most intensely in the mid- to late-twentieth century. Most conservative defenders of inspiration and inerrancy saw the two as inseparable: since God inspired the Bible as his word and because God cannot make errors, the Bible as the word of God must be inerrant. Many nonconservatives who espoused some form of inspiration denied inerrancy, preferring to claim no more than that Scripture "is the only infallible rule of faith and practice." The inerrancy issues in the modern age ranged from defining the term to examining how the Bible views itself to determining the place for biblical criticism. Contemporary readers, looking in on the debate through the written words of those most involved, will see what only some of the contestants observed at the time—that what was ultimately at stake was the very authority and sufficiency of Scripture.

SOURCES ON INERRANCY

These are listed in the order of quotation in this chapter.

Robert D. Preus, "Notes on the Inerrancy of Scripture."

Clark H. Pinnock with Barry L. Callen, *The Scripture Principle*.

Paul D. Feinberg, "The Meaning of Inerrancy."

J. I. Packer, *"Fundamentalism" and the Word of God*.

Stephen T. Davis, *The Debate about the Bible: Inerrancy versus Infallibility.*

E. J. Young, *Thy Word Is Truth.*

James Barr, *Fundamentalism.*

John Murray, "The Attestation of Scripture."

B. B. Warfield, "The Inerrancy of the Original Autographs."

Fisher Humphreys, "Biblical Inerrancy: A Guide for the Perplexed."

John H. Skilton, "The Transmission of the Scriptures."

Harold Lindsell, *The Battle for the Bible.*

Dewey M. Beegle, *The Inspiration of Scripture.*

Carl F. H. Henry, *God, Revelation and Authority*, Vol. 4, *The God Who Speaks and Shows.*

A. A. Hodge and B. B. Warfield, "Inspiration."

R. A. Torrey, *Is the Bible the Inerrant Word of God?*

George Eldon Ladd, *The New Testament and Criticism.*

DOES INSPIRATION DEMAND INERRANCY?

Chapters 1 and 2 covered the inspiration of Scripture. In the controversy over the Bible, contenders across the board adopted some form of the doctrine. The question that arose was, does God's inspiration of the Bible also demand that it be free from error? Some said the two doctrines were inseparably linked; others affirmed inspiration while denying inerrancy. In the following excerpts, Robert D. Preus and Clark H. Pinnock take opposing stands on this matter. Preus asserts a straightforward, conservative, inerrantist position. Pinnock wrestles with the complexity of claiming errorlessness for the Bible. Together they demonstrate that the discussion involved not only the questions of inspiration and inerrancy but biblical authority.

Robert D. Preus, "Notes on the Inerrancy of Scripture" (1984)

The basis of inerrancy rests on the nature of Scripture as God's word. Inerrancy is an inextricable concomitant of inspiration. Our conviction is that since Scripture is truly and properly speaking

God's word, it will not deceive nor err. Admittedly, this is an inference (as in the case of the doctrine of the Trinity or the two natures
of Christ), but it is a necessary inference, because God is faithful
and his word (Scripture) is truth, and no Christian theologian until
the period of rationalism ever shrank from this inference. It is to be
noted that both Christ and the apostles drew the same inference (cf.
not only John 10:35; Mark 12:24; Matt. 5:18-19, but also Christ's
and the apostles' use of the OT: They simply cite it as uncondition-
ally true and unassailable).[1]

Clark H. Pinnock with Barry L. Callen, The Scripture Principle
(1984, 2006)

Finally, what does the Bible teach in regard to the claimed errorlessness of the biblical text, an issue debated so vehemently today,
especially in North America? If God be the author of the Bible, does
it not follow that the text must be free from any flaw and from all
error? Can God lie? Did not Jesus use the Old Testament with such
a total trust as to imply the total perfection of it? The argument from
the nature of God linked to the evidence of the New Testament doctrine of inspiration appears to settle the issue decisively for many.
But the case for biblical errorlessness is not as good as it looks. . . .

From the affirmation of the inspiration of the Bible, we cannot
deduce what the Bible must be like in detail. This leaves us with the
question, Does the New Testament, and did Jesus, teach the perfect
errorlessness of the Scriptures? No, not in plain terms. . . . It is not
just that the term "inerrancy" is not used in the Bible. That would
not settle anything. The point is that the category of inerrancy as
used today is quite a technical one and difficult to define exactly.
It is postulated of the original texts of Scripture no longer extant;
it is held not to apply to round numbers, grammatical structures,
or incidental details in texts and to be unfalsifiable except by some
indisputable argument.

---

[1]Robert D. Preus, "Notes on the Inerrancy of Scripture," *Evangelicals and Inerrancy: Selections
from the Journal of the Evangelical Theological Society*, ed. Ronald Youngblood (Nashville:
Thomas Nelson, 1984), 93.

Once we recall how complex a hypothesis inerrancy is, it is obvious that the Bible teaches no such thing explicitly. What it claims, as we have seen, is divine inspiration and a general reliability, with a distinct concentration on the covenantal revelation of God. And when we examine the text in detail and note how the Gospels differ from one another, how freely the New Testament quotes from the Old Testament, and how boldly the chronicler changes what lay before him in Kings, this impression is strongly confirmed.

Why, then, do some scholars insist that the Bible does claim total inerrancy for itself? Some argue for inerrancy sincerely, hoping that it is true. They find reassurance in this hope. Some ask honestly, How would it be possible to maintain a firm stand against religious liberalism unless one held to total inerrancy? The logic of inspiration coupled with the demands of faith today were quite enough to convince some. Even so, looking at the actual biblical evidence available, we have to conclude that the case for total inerrancy just is not there. At the very most, one could say only that it is implicit and could be drawn out by careful argument, but this is disputable and not the basis for the dogmatic claims one often hears for inerrancy. In the last analysis, the inerrancy theory is a logical deduction not well supported exegetically. Those who press it hard are, in our judgment, elevating reason over Scripture.[2]

INERRANCY DEFINED

Roughly between the 1960s and late 1980s, inerrancy was the prominent topic of discussion among conservative evangelicals concerned by the theological direction of the mainstream Protestant churches. Evangelical inerrantists sought not only to defend inerrancy but to clearly and specifically articulate what they meant by the term. Rather than debate the definition, modernist critics dispensed with the concept, preferring instead what they considered the freer and more flexible term, *infallibility*. Even within conservative circles, several inerrantists, while accepting the word *inerrancy*, admitted their dislike of it because of the comprehensive qualification it neces-

---

[2]Clark H. Pinnock with Barry L. Callen, *The Scripture Principle: Reclaiming the Full Authority of the Bible*, 2nd ed. (Grand Rapids, MI: Baker, 2006), 83–85.

sitated and its negative approach.[3] Paul D. Feinberg, then professor at Trinity Evangelical Divinity School, spoke for most conservative evangelicals at the time with his definition in the excerpt below.[4]

Paul D. Feinberg, "The Meaning of Inerrancy" (1980)

But what is needed, I think, is a more clear and precise definition of inerrancy rather than a new term. People surely accept or reject a word without agreeing with or even knowing what someone else means by it.

It seems to me that the key concept both in the Scriptures and in the minds of those who use the term is truthfulness. Inerrancy has to do with *truth*. Hence, the positive side of the negative idea is that if the Bible is *inerrant*, it is *wholly true*. If this is the case, there are two ways in which the idea could be preserved. First, we could drop the term *inerrant* from the list of preferred terminology and substitute *always true and never false*. Rather than saying, "I believe the Bible is inerrant," we could say, "I believe the Bible is always or wholly true and never false." Second, we could continue using *inerrant* and clearly specify that it is always to be associated with *truth*.

Since the second is more likely to have widespread use, let me propose this definition of inerrancy. *Inerrancy means that when all facts are known, the Scriptures in their original autographs and properly interpreted will be shown to be wholly true in everything that they affirm, whether that has to do with doctrine or morality or with the social, physical, or life sciences.*[5]

INERRANCY AND INFALLIBILITY

Through the nineteenth century, little or no distinction was made between the terms *inerrancy* and *infallibility*. The latter was much more

---

[3]Not least among the evangelicals uncomfortable with the term *inerrancy* was J. I. Packer. For more on this, see Chapter 2 in his *"Fundamentalism" and the Word of God* and his foreword in James Montgomery Boice, *Does Inerrancy Matter?* (Oakland, CA: International Council on Biblical Inerrancy, 1979).
[4]Note the strong similarities between Feinberg's definition and the ICBI's definition in their Chicago Statement on Biblical Inerrancy located in Appendix 1 of this book.
[5]Paul D. Feinberg, "The Meaning of Inerrancy," in *Inerrancy*, ed. Norman L. Geisler (Grand Rapids, MI: Zondervan, 1980), 293–294.

prevalent in the writings of Hodge, Warfield, and others to convey both the trustworthiness and errorlessness of the Bible. In twentieth-century discussions on the doctrine of Scripture, however, both inerrantists and their critics sought to clarify the two terms. For conservatives, both inerrancy and infallibility were affirmed; for liberals and many moderates, infallibility was accepted while inerrancy was rejected. In the segments below, theologian J. I. Packer and philosopher Stephen T. Davis present related but distinct definitions of the terms and opposing views on what evangelicals should affirm about both.

J. I. Packer, "Fundamentalism" and the Word of God (1958)

"Infallible" denotes the quality of never deceiving or misleading, and so means "wholly trustworthy and reliable"; "inerrant" means "wholly true." Scripture is termed infallible and inerrant to express the conviction that all its teaching is the utterance of God "who cannot lie," whose word, once spoken, abides forever, and that therefore it may be trusted implicitly. This is just the conviction about Scripture which our Lord was expressing when he said, "The Scripture cannot be broken," and "it is easier for heaven and earth to pass, than one tittle of the law to fail." God's word is affirmed to be infallible because God himself is infallible; the infallibility of Scripture is simply the infallibility of God speaking. What Scripture says is to be received as the infallible word of the infallible God, and to assert biblical inerrancy and infallibility is just to confess faith in (i) the divine origin of the Bible and (ii) the truthfulness and trustworthiness of God. The value of these terms is that they conserve the principle of biblical authority; for statements that are not absolutely true and reliable could not be absolutely authoritative.[6]

Stephen T. Davis, The Debate about the Bible (1977)

The Bible is infallible, as I define the term,[7] but not inerrant. That is, there are historical and scientific errors in the Bible, but I

---

[6] J. I. Packer, *"Fundamentalism" and the Word of God* (Grand Rapids, MI: Eerdmans, 1958), 95–96.
[7] In the first chapter of his book (*The Debate about the Bible: Inerrancy versus Infallibility*

have found none on matters of faith and practice. I do not claim *a priori* that the Bible is or must be infallible, just that I have found it to be so. Perhaps someday it will be shown that the Bible is not infallible. For now I can only affirm infallibility as the most probable interpretation of the evidence I see. . . .

Normally this term [infallibility] is synonymous with the word "inerrant," but I have offered my own technical definitions and have not used these two terms synonymously. Thus it would not be true to say that biblical infallibility, as I understand this concept, is so close in meaning to biblical inerrancy as to be virtually indistinguishable from it. The person who affirms infallibility does not necessarily believe that every statement made by the biblical writers is true, nor does he feel any need to write books or articles defending everything the Bible says. . . .

It might be asked whether my doctrine of biblical infallibility provides as solid a way of assuring the truth of the major Christian doctrines as biblical inerrancy is designed to do. In one sense the answer to this is yes, for if I am correct that the Bible is infallible, then if a given doctrine can be shown both to be taught in the Bible and to be crucially relevant to Christian faith and practice, that doctrine is true. But in another sense the answer is no, for I affirm biblical infallibility not as a theological *a priori*—i.e., because the doctrine is needed for some theological or apologetic reason—but simply because this seems to be a good way to describe the Bible. The Bible I read just does seem to me infallible, as I define the term. But I am open at any point to the possibility that the Bible is not infallible. Perhaps some future argument or discovery will ruin my doctrine of biblical infallibility. I hope this does not happen, but I agree with Fuller[8] that induction requires leaving the possibility open. Thus, whatever "epistemological basis" infallibility provides

[Philadelphia: Westminster, 1977]), Davis offers this definition of infallibility: "The Bible is infallible if and only if it makes no false or misleading statements on any matter of faith or practice," 23.

[8]Davis refers to the argument made by Daniel P. Fuller in the articles "Benjamin B. Warfield's View of Faith and History," *Bulletin of the Evangelical Theological Society* 11.2 (Spring 1968): 77–82 and "The Nature of Biblical Inerrancy," *Journal of the American Scientific Affiliation* 24 (June 1972): 47–51.

for other doctrines is contingent upon our continued ability rationally to maintain that the Bible is infallible.[9]

THE DANGER OF AN ERRANT BIBLE

In the following selection, the strong inerrantist E. J. Young, then professor of Old Testament at Westminster Theological Seminary, issues a warning to all who would assert that the Bible contains errors. To do so, Young contends, is both arrogant and a serious charge against the veracity of God.

E. J. Young, Thy Word Is Truth (1957)

The Bible, according to its own claims, is breathed forth from God. To maintain that there are flaws or errors in it is the same as declaring that there are flaws or errors in God himself. . . .

When we meet difficulties in Scripture, it is well to be cautious about asserting the presence of error. We as Bible believers are not called upon to offer an answer to all the problems in the Bible any more than we are called upon to offer an explanation of the doctrine of the Trinity. It is perfectly true that our responsibility is to study the biblical difficulties in order, if possible, to understand and to harmonize them. To explain them to everyone's satisfaction, however, or to provide a harmony in every instance, is not incumbent upon us. Hence, if in the light of our present state of knowledge there are some passages which we cannot yet harmonize, we need not become overly discouraged. . . .

It must also be remembered that the mere fact that we ourselves are unable to solve every difficulty and to answer every question does not involve the conclusion that therefore these difficulties are incapable of solution. One reason why we are unable to solve some of the biblical difficulties may simply lie in the fact that we do not know all the factors involved. It is quite conceivable that with the increase of knowledge we may see the answer to some problems which for the present baffle and deny explanation. It is well, when

---

[9]Davis, *The Debate about the Bible*, 115–116, 117, 119–120.

we cannot explain, merely to allow the matter to stand. We have no right to declare that there is no answer. To say the least, such a conclusion involves considerable conceit. We cannot see the explanation of a particular problem; does it therefore follow that there is no answer? Such a conclusion is certainly not consonant with the biblical doctrine of inspiration.[10]

HOW DOES THE BIBLE VIEW ITSELF?

The inerrancy debate drove individuals from all sides back to the Bible in an attempt to determine what, if anything, Scripture claims about itself. Does the Bible take a stand on the quality or extent of its own reliability? In the segments below, James Barr and John Murray present opposing interpretations regarding biblical claims to inerrancy. While these are only two arguments among many on the topic, most theologians involved in the debate either sided with Barr's position[11] or Murray's.[12] Both excerpts contain important keys to each side of the debate. Barr denies an inherent unity to the Bible. Murray considers the strongest case for inerrancy to be the testimony of Jesus to Scripture.

James Barr, Fundamentalism (1977)

According to conservative arguments, it is not only Jesus who made "claims"; the Bible made "claims" about itself. The book of Daniel "claims" to have been written by a historical Daniel some time in the sixth century BC; the book of Deuteronomy "claims" to have been written by Moses; and more important still, the Bible as a whole "claims" to be divinely inspired. All this is nonsense. There is no "the Bible" that "claims" to be divinely inspired, there is no

---

[10]E. J. Young, *Thy Word Is Truth* (Grand Rapids, MI: Eerdmans, 1957), 123–125.

[11]Similarly to Barr, James D. G. Dunn concludes that the Bible does not consider itself inerrant; see his "The Authority of Scripture According to Scripture," *Churchman: A Journal of Anglican Theology* 96 (1982): 107–113, 118. Also note that Pinnock agrees with this position in the excerpt from *The Scripture Principle* at the beginning of this chapter.

[12]For similar treatments of this topic from two other onetime Westminster professors, see John M. Frame, "Scripture Speaks for Itself," in *God's Inerrant Word*, ed. John Warwick Montgomery (Minneapolis: Bethany, 1974), 178–200 and Sinclair B. Ferguson, "How Does the Bible Look at Itself?" in *Inerrancy and Hermeneutic: A Tradition, a Challenge, a Debate,* ed. Harvie M. Conn (Grand Rapids, MI: Baker, 1988), 47–66.

"it" that has a "view of itself." There is only this or that source, like 2 Timothy or 2 Peter, which makes statements about certain other writings, these rather undefined. There is no such thing as "the Bible's view of itself" from which a fully authoritative answer to these questions can be obtained. This whole side of traditional conservative apologetic, though loudly vociferated, just does not exist; there is no case to answer.[13]

John Murray, "The Attestation of Scripture" (1946)

If the Bible does not witness to its own infallibility,[14] then we have no right to believe that it is infallible. If it does bear witness to its infallibility then our faith in it must rest upon that witness, however much difficulty may be entertained with this belief. If this position with respect to the ground of faith in Scripture is abandoned, then appeal to the Bible for the ground of faith in any doctrine must also be abandoned. The doctrine of Scripture must be elicited from the Scripture just as any other doctrine should be. If the doctrine of Scripture is denied its right to appeal to Scripture for its support, then what right does any other doctrine have to make this appeal? . . .

First of all, there is the negative evidence. The Scripture does not adversely criticize itself. One part of Scripture does not expose another part as erroneous. It goes without saying that, if Scripture itself witnessed to the errancy and fallibility of another part, then such witness would be a finality, and belief in the inerrancy of Scripture would have to be abandoned. But it is a signal fact that one Scripture does not predicate error of another. It is true that the Scripture contains the record of much sin and error in the history of men, of Satan and of demons. The Bible, of course, is to a large extent historical in character and, since history is strewn with sin, the Bible could not fail to record the dark and dismal story. Indeed, the frankness and candor of the Bible in this regard is one of its most striking features. The openness with which it exposes even the sins

[13]James Barr, *Fundamentalism* (London: SCM, 1977), 78.
[14]In this article, Murray does not clearly distinguish between inerrancy and infallibility. He, along with most inerrantists of his day, considered them so close in meaning and so inseparably linked that no distinction was necessary.

of the saints is one of the most signal marks of its authenticity. But the condemnation of the sin and error the Bible records is not witness to its own fallibility. It is rather an integral part of the witness to its own credibility and, so far from constituting any evidence against itself as inerrant Scripture, it thereby contributes evidence that is most germane to the establishment of its infallibility. . . .

When we say the witness of the New Testament we mean, of course, the authoritative speakers and writers of the New Testament. First and foremost among such authoritative witnesses is our Lord himself. His word is a finality: on any other supposition the whole superstructure of Christian faith must totter and crumble. What then is our Lord's testimony with respect to the Old Testament? . . .

The inescapable fact is that the mass of direct and indirect statements leads to one conclusion that, for our Lord, the Scripture, just because it was *Scripture*, just because it fell within the denotation of the formula, "it is written," was a finality. His attitude is one of meticulous acceptance and reverence. The only explanation of such an attitude is that what Scripture said, God said, that the Scripture was God's word, that it was God's word because it was Scripture and that it was or became Scripture because it was God's word. That he distinguished between the word of God borne to us by Scripture and the written word itself would be an imposition upon Jesus's own teaching wholly alien to the identification Jesus makes and to the reverence for the letter of Scripture so pervasive in all of his witness.[15]

EXTENT OF INERRANCY

Another subject that received considerable discussion through the nineteenth and twentieth centuries was the extent of the Bible's inerrancy. Among conservative evangelicals, inerrancy of the original manuscripts was accepted (with and without qualification), but questions arose regarding the reliability of the transmission of Scripture through the ages in the forms of copies and translations. Which Bible could be considered inerrant? If we have an

---

[15] John Murray, "The Attestation of Scripture," in *The Infallible Word: A Symposium*, ed. Ned B. Stonehouse and Paul Woolley (Phillipsburg, NJ: P&R, 1946), 8–9, 11, 19–20, 27–28.

errant copy or translation, do we still have the word of God? If our Bible contains errors, is it still sufficient? These were the questions inerrantists wrestled with for their understanding and in defense of biblical inerrancy. The following segments provide a picture of the broad array of inerrantist answers to the question of reliability and trustworthiness. Warfield and Fisher Humphreys contend for the inerrancy of the *original* manuscripts alone. John H. Skilton explains an inerrantist's view on providential care in transmission. Harold Lindsell, from his well-known book *The Battle for the Bible*, explains transmission and defends the reliability of current manuscripts in unmistakable terms.

B. B. Warfield, "The Inerrancy of the Original Autographs" (1893)

It is certainly a curiosity of the controversial use of a phrase, to see the church's *limitation* of her affirmation of the absolute truth and trustworthiness of the Scriptures in all their declarations, to those Scriptures "as they came from God," represented as an additional strain upon faith. Would these controversialists have the church affirm the absolute truth of scribes' slips and printers' errors? If we were to take some of them "at the foot of the letter," they would seem to represent it as easier to believe in the infallibility of compositors and proofreaders than the infallibility of God. Everybody knows that no book was ever printed, much less hand-copied, into which some errors did not intrude in the process; and as we do not hold the author responsible for these in an ordinary book, neither ought we to hold God responsible for them in this extraordinary book which we call the Bible. It is *the Bible* that we declare to be "of infallible truth"—the Bible that God gave us, not the corruptions and slips which scribes and printers have given us, some of which are in every copy. Yet a recent writer,[16] with a great show of solemnity, calls upon the Presbyterian church for "a frank and full disavowal" "of any intention to make the inerrancy of the original autographs (as distinguished from *the Bible as it is*) a test

---

[16]Henry Van Dyke, *The Bible as It Is* (New York: W. C. Martin, 1893).

of orthodoxy." But what is it that distinguishes "the Bible as it is" from the original autographs? Just scribes' corruptions and print- ers' errors; nothing else. And so this controversialist would have the church "frankly and fully" disavow attaching more inerrancy to the word of God, given the inspiration to men, than to the errors and corruptions of careless or bungling scribes and printers! Taken literally, this demand would amount to a strong asseveration of the utter untrustworthiness of the Bible.[17]

Fisher Humphreys, "Biblical Inerrancy" (1987)

No modern text or translation of the Bible is inerrant, only the original Hebrew and Greek manuscripts of the Bible are—or, more accurately, were—inerrant. Modern texts and responsible transla- tions are very trustworthy, of course; but inerrancy is affirmed only for the autographs, that is, the original manuscripts. These manu- scripts, everyone agrees, no longer exist.

This is the most important of the qualifications on inerrancy. It means that the controversy in the SBC[18] does not concern the Bible we have today. It concerns nonexistent ancient manuscripts. Strictly speaking, we probably ought not to speak of the inerrancy of the Bible, since that suggests to most people that we are talking about the Bible as we now have it.[19] Strictly speaking, we should speak of the iner- rancy of the original Hebrew and Greek manuscripts of the Bible.[20]

John H. Skilton, "The Transmission of the Scriptures" (1946)

We will grant that God's care and providence, singular though they have been, have not preserved for us any of the original manu-

[17]B. B. Warfield, "The Inerrancy of the Original Autographs," *Selected Shorter Writings of Benjamin B. Warfield*, 2 vols., ed. John E. Meeter (Phillipsburg, NJ: P&R, 1973), 2:582–583.
[18]The controversy in the Southern Baptist Convention over the inerrancy and authority of the Bible to which Humphreys is referring ran simultaneously to that in the evangelical and larger mainstream Protestant world.
[19]In contrast to Humphreys, Young suggests that there "are extant today many Bibles in many languages of which we may truthfully say that they are the infallible and inerrant word of God, yet of which we cannot say they are inspired," *Thy Word Is Truth*, 146.
[20]Fisher Humphreys, "Biblical Inerrancy: A Guide for the Perplexed," in *The Unfettered Word: Southern Baptists Confront the Authority-Inerrancy Question*, ed. Robison B. James (Waco, TX: Word, 1987), 50.

scripts either of the Old Testament or of the New Testament. We will furthermore grant that God did not keep from error those who copied the Scriptures during the long period in which the sacred text was transmitted in copies written by hand. But we must maintain that the God who gave the Scriptures, who works all things after the counsel of his will, has exercised a remarkable care over his word, has preserved it in all ages in a state of essential purity, and has enabled it to accomplish the purpose for which he gave it. It is inconceivable that the sovereign God who was pleased to give his word as a vital and necessary instrument in the salvation of his people would permit his word to become completely marred in its transmission and unable to accomplish its ordained end. Rather, as surely as that he is God, we would expect to find him exercising a singular care in the preservation of his written revelation.[21]

Harold Lindsell, The Battle for the Bible (1976)

Most evangelical writers and indeed many of the doctrinal statements that support inerrancy speak of it in connection with the autographs, that is, the original Scriptures. No one claims that the autographs exist, and certain questions must be addressed as a result of this. No doubt, God did not intend for the autographs to be preserved. They would have been accorded a treatment similar to that given to the *Granth*, the sacred scriptures of Sikhism. That writing is virtually worshiped and is kept encased in such a way as to place the emphasis on the book rather than on the god who lies behind it. Idolatry is hardly new, and we may be sure that the possession of the original books of Scripture would have been an incipient temptation to idolatrous worship.

God did not shield Scripture when it became a part of history. Moreover he did not shield Adam and Eve in the garden so as to make it impossible for them to disobey their creator. Nor did he shield his son Jesus from the possibility of sin in his humanity. In the history of the Christian church it has been carefully stated that

---

[21]John H. Skilton, "The Transmission of the Scriptures," in *The Infallible Word: A Symposium*, ed. Ned B. Stonehouse and Paul Woolley, 143.

Jesus in his deity was not able to sin, and that Jesus in his humanity was not able to sin. . . . Nor did God choose to preserve the mercy seat that was in the Holy of Holies in the tabernacle and in the temple. It has disappeared. But in the providential care of God, he has preserved the Scriptures for us so that they have remained unadulterated, by which we mean free from error.

Any student of lower criticism[22] admits that there have been copyists' mistakes made by those who diligently sought to reproduce the books of the Bible by hand. But the copyist's mistake is something entirely different from an error in Scripture. A misspelled or a misplaced word is a far cry from error, by which is meant a misstatement or something that is contrary to fact. . . .

It is hardly novel to say that lower criticism has worked through the thousands of manuscripts of the Bible that are available and in the reconstruction of the text scholars have produced a product that can be said to be the word of God. Textual problems today in no way make the doctrine of biblical inerrancy impossible. It must be remembered, too, that those who scoff at the inerrancy of the autographs because they cannot be produced for examination have no better case arguing for the errancy of texts they cannot produce either. At the worst, it is a standoff.

I add one further word about the autographs of Scripture and the copies we now have. Anyone who has doubts about the accuracy of the Scriptures that have come down to us by transmission through copyists is misinformed. We can say honestly that the Bible we have today is the word of God. This is not to deny the existence of textual problems, as we have already said. But the textual problems are minimal. Thus it is, that one of the world's foremost New Testament scholars, F. F. Bruce, has this to say in response to those who claim that infallibility is void because we do not have the original documents, and because of variant readings we cannot get back to them: "The variant readings about which any doubt remains . . . affect no material question of historic fact

---

[22]In today's contemporary biblical studies, the term "lower criticism" has been replaced with "textual criticism" to refer to what Lindsell is describing here.

or of Christian faith and practice."[23] Therefore the variant readings offer no embarrassment to inerrancy advocates, for they do not impinge on the question at the point of the real tension. The places where the chief critics of inerrancy lay their emphases are, for the most part, places where there are no textual problems but where the claim in favor of errancy must be determined wholly apart from variant readings. . . .[24]

TRUSTWORTHY BUT ERRANT?

On the liberal or modernist side of the same issue—the extent of the reliability of the Bible—there was no unified acceptance of inerrancy. There was the precise opposite, a total rejection of errorlessness. The errantist affirmed biblical trustworthiness apart from inerrancy. In the first of the following passages, Dewey M. Beegle admits errors in the Bible, yet defends the biblical text as "authentic, accurate, and trustworthy" in vital matters of faith and practice. In the second passage, Carl F. H. Henry responds to the position held by Beegle, arguing that trustworthiness and inerrancy must both be affirmed together if the Bible's authority is to be retained.

Dewey M. Beegle, The Inspiration of Scripture (1963)

At first the witness of revelation from God was in the form of oral report. In due time some of these reports were reduced to writing, especially the key redemptive, historical events and the compelling "word of the Lord" which came to the prophets. The pattern of oral tradition followed by written records was equally true of the New Testament. In this whole process of transmitting, recording, and compiling the deeds and words of God, the Spirit of God was active in the hearts and minds of God's servants. But this activity did not extend to inerrant transmission, either oral or written, and neither did it guarantee an absolute inerrancy of the original documents. What the Spirit's activity did guarantee was selectivity of

---

[23]F. F. Bruce, *The New Testament Documents: Are They Reliable?* (Leichester, UK: Inter-Varsity, 1960), 14–15.
[24]Harold Lindsell, *The Battle for the Bible* (Grand Rapids, MI: Zondervan, 1976), 36–37.

events and accuracy of reporting and interpretation sufficient to achieve God's purpose throughout the rest of man's existence. . . .

In all essential matters of faith and practice Scripture is authentic, accurate, and trustworthy. It is the indispensable record of revelation, product of inspiration, and source of authority. By Scripture, and it alone, revelation, inspiration, and authority become subjective truth in every earnest heart through the agency of the same Spirit who watched over Scripture's recording and transmission. This result occurs whether Scripture is in the original languages or in translation. Of course, for clarification of specific details, the best extant text of the Hebrew and Aramaic in the Old Testament and the Greek in the New Testament will always have a priority over any translations. But in the great issues of faith (love for God) and action (love for man) Scripture in translation is sufficient to achieve God's purpose. This is true of all translations even though they have unintentional, and in some cases deliberate, variation from the clear text of the extant manuscripts. As far as the translation itself is concerned, and indirectly the reader, the reason for the variation does not matter. Enough of the redemptive truth is woven throughout Scripture that the Holy Spirit can take any translation and use it for the salvation of the sincere reader.[25]

Carl F. H. Henry, *God, Revelation and Authority* (1979)

[A]ny emphasis only on biblical trustworthiness in distinction from scriptural inerrancy involves a measure of ambiguity and may in fact embrace also a significant shift in the conception of scriptural authority. The Bible merits confidence, on this view, because of its dependability; it is fit or worthy to be relied on, that is, of proven consistency in producing satisfactory results. But unless such conceptions of trustworthiness and reliability include a cognitive claim for the objective truthfulness of the Bible, they seem to deploy the emphasis from intellectual to volitional concerns. The governing issue is whether the Bible is reliably

---

[25]Dewey M. Beegle, *The Inspiration of Scripture* (Philadelphia: Westminster, 1963), 190, 192. Beegle later revised and updated his work, publishing it in 1973 under the title *Scripture, Tradition, and Infallibility.*

truthful. Is it then trustworthy not simply in respect to salvific efficacy but also as objectively inspired truth? Some mediating thinkers emphasize that Scripture is not a source of truth in matters of history, science, geography, and so on. But can the Bible be comprehensively trusted, that is, can it be considered truly reliable, if an acceptance of truth of some of its teaching would commit us to error? Unless one deprives biblical truth of an objectively valid and sharable content, and transmutes it into an internal faith-stance, can we . . . hold on the one hand that the biblical writers are not vehicles of revelatory truth in matters other than salvation, while on the other hand we affirm the Bible's infallibility?[26]

INERRANCY AND HUMAN LIMITATIONS

Closely related to biblical reliability is the relationship between inerrancy and the human writers of the Bible. As in the discussion on inspiration, the nature of the interaction between the divine and the human is paramount. Faced with the relationship, critics of inerrancy disavowed themselves from what they considered the rigid doctrine of verbal inspiration. The best of the inerrantists, however, fully recognized the freedom and fallibility of the human writers of Scripture and still held to inerrancy. In another excerpt from their classic article, "Inspiration," Hodge and Warfield defend the inerrancy of the biblical text in conjunction with the humanity of its authors.

A. A. Hodge and B. B. Warfield, "Inspiration" (1881)

The writers of this article are sincerely convinced of the perfect soundness of the great catholic doctrine of biblical inspiration, i.e., that the Scriptures not only contain, but *are the word of God*, and hence that all their elements and all their affirmations are absolutely errorless, and binding the faith and obedience of men. Nevertheless we admit that the question between ourselves and the advocates of the view just stated, is one of fact, to be decided only by an exhaustive and impartial examination of all the sources of evidence, i.e., the claims and the phenomena of the Scriptures themselves. There will

---

[26]Carl F. H. Henry, *God, Revelation and Authority*, 4 vols. (Waco, TX: Word, 1979), 4:170.

undoubtedly be found upon the surface many apparent affirmations presumably inconsistent with the present teachings of science, with facts of history, or with other statements of the sacred books themselves. Such apparent inconsistencies and collisions with other sources of information are to be expected in imperfect copies of ancient writings; from the fact that the original reading may have been lost, or that we are destitute of the circumstantial knowledge which would fill up and harmonize the record. Besides, the human forms of knowledge by which the critics test the accuracy of Scripture are themselves subject to error. In view of all the facts known to us, we affirm that a candid inspection of all the ascertained phenomena of the original text of Scripture will leave unmodified the ancient faith of the church. In all their real affirmations these books are without error.

It must be remembered that it is not claimed that the Scriptures any more than their authors are omniscient. The information they convey is in the forms of human thought, and limited on all sides. They were not designed to teach philosophy, science, or human history as such. They were not designed to furnish an infallible system of speculative theology. They are written in human languages, whose words, inflections, constructions, and idioms bear everywhere indelible traces of human error. The record itself furnishes evidence that the writers were in large measure dependent for their knowledge upon sources and methods in themselves fallible; and that their personal knowledge and judgments were in many matters hesitating and defective, or even wrong. Nevertheless the historical faith of the church has always been, that all the affirmations of Scriptures of all kinds, whether of spiritual doctrine or duty, or of physical or historical fact, or of psychological or philosophical principle, are without any error, when the *ipsissima verba* of the original autographs are ascertained and interpreted in their natural and intended sense. There is a vast difference between exactness of statement, which includes an exhaustive rendering of details, an absolute literalness, which the Scriptures never profess, and accuracy, on the other hand, which secures a correct statement of facts or principles intended to be affirmed. It is this accuracy and this alone, as distinct from exactness, which the church doctrine maintains of every affirmation in the original text of Scripture without exception. Every statement accurately corresponds to truth just as far forth as affirmed.[27]

INERRANCY AND CRITICISM

Perhaps the strongest words in the inerrancy controversy were used by the strict inerrantists in their clash with biblical criticism. In the first two selections, R. A. Torrey and E. J. Young denounce critical studies that undermine the authority of Scripture. In the final passage George Eldon Ladd attempts to moderate between an inerrantist position that tends toward literalism and a higher-critical method that approaches the Bible merely as a flawed historical document.

R. A. Torrey, Is the Bible the Inerrant Word of God? (1922)

Twenty-five or thirty years ago, I was talking with a good man and a sound man, but not a very clear and far-seeing thinker, about the destructive criticism as it stood then. He said to me, in speaking of some of the more mildly destructive theories, "They tell me it does not touch any vital point anyway, and what difference does it make whether Isaiah wrote the later chapters of the book or whether someone else wrote them?" I told him that this was only the entering wedge, and I urged him to look to where it would lead and where it would end. It has led to and ended exactly where I then predicted it would. Any smallest insect of destructive criticism is like the little borer ant which gets into the underpinning of Hawaiian houses and bores and bores away unseen, until suddenly the whole house collapses. Believe the Bible, *believe the whole Bible.* It will prove in the ultimate outcome every time that it is either the whole Bible or else no Bible at all. . . .

But exactly what is involved in believing the whole Bible?

In the first place, *believe its every statement, its historical state-*

---

[27]A. A. Hodge and B. B. Warfield, "Inspiration," *The Presbyterian Review* 2 (April 1881): 237–238.

ments, its doctrinal statements, its statements of every kind. Every statement that the Bible makes (that is, the Bible as originally given) is absolutely true. Of course, as we have seen in a recent sermon, that does not mean that every statement that every one is recorded in the Bible as making is necessarily true, for, as we saw then, the Bible records some statements that the devil made and uninspired men made, but the Bible statement that the devil or these uninspired men made these statements is absolutely true.[28]

E. J. Young, *Thy Word Is Truth* (1957)

One thing that stands out immediately is that the Bible which is being rediscovered is the Bible of "criticism," and not of historic Christianity. This is to be expected, inasmuch as it is impossible for men to hold the principles of higher criticism, as it has been practiced by those who reject the infallibility of Scripture, and at the same time arrive at the position of evangelical Christianity. A man may practice the principles of criticism or he may be a believer in evangelical Christianity. One thing, however, is clear: if he is consistent, he cannot possibly espouse both. Either he will practice the principles of "criticism" or else he will follow a Christian method of study. If he follows the principles of "criticism," these principles will not lead him to evangelical Christianity. If he is an ardent believer in evangelical Christianity, he will not want to follow the principles of "criticism." Consequently, we must note well that the modern scholar who is unwilling to abandon the principles which characterized so much of the Bible study during the nineteenth century cannot and does not arrive at the position of historic orthodox Christianity. The orthodox terminology which is so frequently employed today by modern theologians means something quite different from that which the humble Bible believer would expect it to mean. The Bible which modern scholarship is presenting to us is quite different from that infallible word to which the Christian has been accustomed to turn to hear the voice of God.[29]

---

[28]R. A. Torrey, *Is the Bible the Inerrant Word of God?* (New York: George H. Doran, 1922), 92–93.
[29]Young, *Thy Word is Truth*, 218–219.

George Eldon Ladd, The New Testament and Criticism (1967)

Thus the Bible is indeed the inspired word of God, the Christian's only infallible rule for faith and practice. But the present study [of biblical criticism] has attempted to demonstrate that the truth of infallibility does not extend to the preservation of an infallible text, nor to an infallible lexicography, nor to infallible answers to all questions about authorship, date, sources, etc., nor to an infallible reconstruction of the historical situation in which revelatory events occurred and the books of the Bible were written. Such questions God in his providence has committed to human scholarship to answer; and often the answers must be imperfect and tentative. A proper evangelical, biblical faith suffers a severe disservice when the spheres of biblical authority and critical judgment are confused.

Although the truth of the Bible is not dependent upon our ability to answer critical questions, it is quite clear that our understanding of the truth of the Bible is enlarged and rendered more precise by such study. A proper biblical criticism therefore does not mean criticizing the word of God but trying to understand the word of God and how it has been given to man. . . .

The critical study of the Bible is necessary, not to grasp its saving power to speak to men of the redemption that is in Jesus Christ, or to bring them through Christ to God, but to answer questions about the historical process by which God has given us his word. To be sure, there are innumerable places where the spiritual message of the Bible will be far better understood when its historical setting is disclosed, and for this reason the layman should constantly seek the aid of helps in biblical study prepared by good scholars; and scholars should not neglect the preparing of such scholarly but non-technical tools for laymen. However, it must not be forgotten that such critical study involves the effort to recover a complex historical process now often lost to us. Therefore the conclusions of scholars will often differ from each other; certainty often cannot be obtained. Nevertheless, critical study has shed a flood of light upon our understanding of the New Testament.[30]

---

[30]George Eldon Ladd, *The New Testament and Criticism* (Grand Rapids, MI: Eerdmans, 1967), 216–218.

5

Biblical authority is an empty notion unless we know how to determine what the Bible means.

J. I. PACKER

When I use a word it means just what I choose it to mean, neither more nor less.

HUMPTY DUMPTY, AS QUOTED IN LEWIS CARROLL'S
THROUGH THE LOOKING GLASS

The interesting thing about culture shifts is that they are not marked on some calendar, not programmed to occur. Instead, they just happen. To be sure, certain events can trigger seismic shifts. Luther posted his Ninety-Five Theses, a seismic shift eventually resulting in the Protestant Reformation, due in part to the celebration of All Souls' Day in the castle church at Wittenberg. Luther didn't, however, set out to begin Protestantism that day. When Rome was sacked, the glory days of the Greco-Roman era came to an end. When Copernicus and Isaac Newton made their discoveries, the way in which the world was to be understood would be forever changed. Events can give shape to culture shifts, to paradigm shifts. But still, such cultural change isn't programmed, isn't scheduled. It just happens.

During the closing decades of the twentieth century, such a

cultural shift likely took place. Although there is much debate over specifics, there is a growing consensus that modernism gave way to postmodernism as the twentieth century was coming to a close. Some do not see it this way. Instead, they prefer to see the contemporary moment as ultra-modernism. The prevailing opinion nevertheless is that we are in the postmodern age. Much debate surrounds when postmodernism began and surrounds its true identity. The debate is bogged down by those who are quick to point out that dating things and naming, classifying, and quantifying them are activities belonging to modernism, while postmodernism eschews such activities. Despite all of the debate and dissonance, again the prevailing notion is that we are now living in the postmodern age, and whatever that means in its entirety it at least means this: we are in a different cultural climate. As expressed by the words of a recent country song ("A Different World" by Bucky Covington), this isn't just a different time from the past, it's a different place. It is a different cultural place. This culture shift has not passed the doctrine of Scripture by.

In addition to the doctrines of inspiration and inerrancy getting significant attention since the mid-1850s on to the present day, the limelight has shone on the interpretation of Scripture as well. The technical term for interpreting texts is hermeneutics, from the Greek name Hermes, who acted as messenger for the gods in Greek mythology. While finding the meaning of biblical texts has always been crucial business for the church, there certainly have been more books written on hermeneutics in the modern age than at any other time in the life of the church. Hermeneutics is typically defined as the art and science of biblical interpretation. From the mid-nineteenth century on it has seen its fair share of attention and development as a science, as a technical discipline. Many Christian organizations and some churches have a statement regarding hermeneutics in their doctrinal statements. Even the Chicago Statement on Scripture by the International Council on Biblical Inerrancy includes articles on interpretation.

While there is much debate over proper hermeneutical method

and the rules of interpretation, and greater debate still over differing interpretations of biblical texts once those methods are applied, there tends to be little self-reflection about this whole practice of and emphasis on hermeneutics. We tend to give very little thought to the way we read texts, biblical texts or other texts. We just read them. Seminary students and graduate students in literature, philosophy, and history may be the exception, but they are the exception that proves the rule. This chapter asks the question of how we read the biblical text and why we read the biblical text the ways that we do. This chapter takes a step back, if you will, to analyze the cultural context(s) that have produced all of this hermeneutical work and thought. Further still, this chapter looks at biblical interpretation in light of the dawning of postmodernism.

THINKING OF TEXTS

In his 2006 presidential address to the Evangelical Theological Society, Edwin Yamauchi proposed three ways that evangelicals tend to read the Bible. It is read, he cleverly observed, as either talisman, specimen, or dragoman. The talisman approach turns the text into a lucky charm. Texts become magical spells that one can dangle over a problem or a challenging situation. The text as specimen reflects the opposite approach. This is the critical approach to the text. One envisions lab coats and scientists coolly and detachedly dissecting the text, debating its meaning, and displaying the results in a scholarly paper. Yamauchi was addressing a room full of professional biblical scholars and theologians, those who could potentially tend not to see the text as talisman but as specimen, those who write textbooks on the *science* of biblical interpretation, and those who debate the meaning of texts. Yamauchi prefers Scripture as dragoman "or 'interpreter.'" Like Scripture as specimen, this approach also represents "the scholarly study of Scripture," but it is by believers who seek guidance from the text, guidance for today.[1]

---

[1] The address was given by Edwin M. Yamauchi at the 2006 ETS meeting in Washington D.C. and was published as "Scripture as Talisman, Specimen, or Dragoman," *Journal of the Evangelical Theological Society* 50:1 (March 1, 2007), 3–30.

Higher criticism evolved from the seedbed of modernism, a cultural mood that gave prominence to the hard sciences and stressed rationalism, a worldview that looked at nearly everything, even human beings, as specimens. The discipline of history, in order to be respected as an academic discipline in this brave new world, became hemmed in by the rules of scientific investigation. The Bible is after all history. Modernist biblical scholars applied these rules of scientific investigation to the text. In the process, matters of faith became immediately suspect. The laws of nature govern the universe. Miracles are by nature the suspension of such laws. Therefore, the logic goes, miracles simply don't happen. The fact that the Bible contains miracles simply points to its mythological character, the fact that it is an ancient text written by and for ancient people. Moderns need to read the Bible too, though. Higher criticism helps separate the dross, which includes things like miracles, the trappings of the mythological worldview, from the gold, the eternal abiding witness to God and eternal, abiding truth. Higher criticism made the Bible acceptable to moderns. That much has been the story of modernism and liberalism told in the previous chapters.

A question remains, however: does modernism influence the theologically conservative side of biblical studies and biblical interpretation? Yamauchi's discussion of the text as specimen might suggest, uncomfortably to be sure, the affirmative.

This is not to suggest that hermeneutics as a discipline and hermeneutical or exegetical debates are unhealthy or mere products of slavish captivity to modernism. Sound hermeneutic theory and practice are crucial to the church, since bad interpretations lead to bad theology and bad theology leads to bad practice. The gospel and the church's witness and vitality suffer when bad interpretations flourish. It is to suggest, however, that questions of self-examination—why do we read texts the way we do?—and a little self-criticism—how can I read the text better?—go a long way in helping us become more faithful disciples of Christ.

RULES OF ENGAGEMENT

Just as they played a formative role in the doctrines of inspiration and inerrancy, the Princetonians also played a formative role in the practice of interpretation. In his magisterial *Systematic Theology*, a text that ruled as a textbook in seminaries when it first came out and still gets assigned today, Charles Hodge laid out the "Rules of Interpretation," three rules to be exact. Hodge describes these rules as being "not arbitrary. They are not imposed by human authority. They have no binding force which does not flow from their own intrinsic truth and propriety."[2] Hodge is making the point that these are objective rules, undeniable facts. The three rules are simply that Scripture is to be interpreted in its "plain and historical sense," that "Scripture cannot contradict Scripture," and that Scripture is "to be interpreted under the guidance of the Holy Spirit." Each of these needs a little unpacking.

The first, the plain, historical sense of the text, stands counter to a long-reigning view of interpretation referred to as the allegorical method. This hermeneutical approach, popular in the early church and medieval era, looked for deeper meaning underlying the literal or surface meaning of the text. Hodge reflects the tendency away from such allegorical readings toward the plain, historical meaning of the text. The twentieth century would expand this rule, as will be seen shortly. The second rule, involving Scripture interpreting Scripture, reflects the so-called analogy of faith, a long-held rule and practice in the church. Since God is the author of Scripture, Scripture cannot contradict itself. In practical terms this means that when the meaning of a particular text is obscure or a bit foggy, other more clear texts should be used to help make sense of it. Augustine took this a step further, claiming that the Apostles' Creed stands as the "Rule of Faith," a boundary or guardrail within which our interpretations of Scripture must remain.[3] Finally, in the third rule, Hodge reminds his readers that interpreting Scripture is not merely a scientific enterprise; it is a spiritual one.

---

[2] Charles Hodge, *Systematic Theology*, 3 vols. (Grand Rapids, MI: Eerdmans, 1872–1873), 187.
[3] "Rule of Faith," *Augustine through the Ages: An Encyclopedia*, ed. Allan D. Fitzgerald (Grand Rapids, MI: Eerdmans, 1999).

Hodge's first rule received a great deal of attention and development. Yet those following Hodge tend to point out that hermeneutical rules aren't imposed. In the words of Walter Kaiser, "The general principles of interpreting are not learned, invented, or discovered by people. They are part and parcel of the nature of man as a being in the image of God."[4] We are by nature interpreters, runs this argument. Biblical scholars and authors of hermeneutics textbooks aren't inventing or discovering rules of interpretation. But they are naming them. The names they arrived at, since Hodge first put forth his rule of the "plain, historical sense," include grammatical, historical, literary or rhetorical, and canonical. Sometimes this is simply put forth as the grammatical-historical interpretation of the text.

Vern S. Poythress explains this approach: "Interpretation of the Bible involves both a linguistic side, focusing on the language of the Bible, and a historical side, focusing on the events and the contexts in which they occur."[5] The grammatical side entails the exegesis of the text, the analysis of the text in its original languages, its parts of speech, its grammatical or clausal connections, and the meaning of the words. The historical side entails issues of geography and history, as well as issues of cultural customs and practices. The interpreter of the text, especially the modern interpreter of the text, is in one sense removed from the text. The biblical text speaks of ancient places and ancient times, ancient customs and practices, all conveyed in ancient languages. It falls to the modern interpreter to somehow reconstruct the world of the biblical text to understand its meaning.

This approach to hermeneutics has some presuppositions behind it. One presupposition, at a very basic level, is that texts have meaning. Another presupposition is that texts have a *particular* meaning that can be arrived at objectively. This presupposition results in a hermeneutical practice that seeks to uncover the author's intended meaning. Speaking of literary texts in general and not in specific

---

[4]Walter C. Kaiser Jr., "Legitimate Hermeneutics," in *A Guide to Contemporary Hermeneutics: Major Trends in Biblical Interpretation*, ed. Donald K. McKim (Grand Rapids, MI: Eerdmans, 1986), 114.
[5]Vern S. Poythress, *God-Centered Biblical Interpretation* (Phillipsburg, NJ: P&R, 1999), 164.

reference to the Bible, E. D. Hirsch made the point that the best meaning is the author's meaning. Otherwise, the literary critic, in arriving at a meaning at odds with the author's, becomes the "author" of the meaning. We should enter into, in Hirsch's terminology, the author's "horizon" through the grammatical-historical hermeneutic to arrive at the meaning of the text. In order to do so, we need to push our own horizon to the margins so we can focus on the author's horizon.[6]

In the context of modernism, another presupposition lurks around the edges here, that of objectivity and neutrality in interpretation. If interpretation is turned into a scientific discipline—think of lab coats—then the interpreter becomes a detached figure, applying a method to arrive at the "right" meaning. The more the interpreter gets in the way, the less objective the interpreter, the more difficulty there is in arriving at the right meaning of the text. This is, of course, a caricature. But it does reveal something about the way texts are read in a framework of modernism. Vern Poythress points to an underlying flaw in this modernist assumption: science is not neutral or objective since, primarily, science is done by scientists. Poythress observes, "Until recently, most people have thought that science presented a totally objective analysis of the facts. But recent examination of the history of science has cast doubt on this assumption."[7]

The casting of aspersions on the scientific method is not to suggest its outright rejection. Instead, it serves as a cautionary tale not to put undue faith in the method. The reality is that the interpreter is not neutral but rather comes to the text from a context. Rather than assume that the horizon of the reader can be pushed to the margins, it might be better to acknowledge the interplay between the two horizons. In his text on hermeneutics, *The Hermeneutical Spiral*, Grant Osborne makes the case that as we acknowledge our

---

[6]E. D. Hirsch, *Validity in Interpretation* (New Haven, CT: Yale University Press, 1967). A similar view was put forth in the book written for a more popular audience—Mortimer J. Adler, *How to Read a Book* (New York: Touchstone, 1972).
[7]Vern S. Poythress, *Science and Hermeneutics*, reprinted in *Foundations of Contemporary Interpretation: Six Volumes in One*, ed. Moisés Silva (Grand Rapids, MI: Zondervan, 1996), 442.

horizon as the reader, we come to the text with a higher degree of honesty. He also makes the point that as we peer into the text, the text becomes a mirror of us. The response Osborne hopes for is one of submission and correction of our own horizon in light of the text, not the other way around. This approach understands the hermeneutical process as a process, a spiral up to greater and clearer understanding of the text.[8]

There may have been the tendency, in the earlier stages of the development of the grammatical-historical hermeneutic, to assume a certain neutrality and objectivity, to put a little too much faith in the method. These recent developments have simply called attention to the presuppositions we all bring to the text; interpretation, in the words of Anthony Thiselton, involves two horizons.[9] One further development of the grammatical-historical method is the attention given to genre. The Bible, Tremper Longman argues, is "self-conscious about form," about "artful verbal expression." In other words, the Bible is literature, with poetry and narrative, the apocalyptic and prophetic, the didactic and prose. Longman and many others have argued that approaching the Bible as literature, being sensitive to the various conventions of the various genres, can be quite helpful in understanding the text. The literary approach has led to the expansion of the term grammatical-historical to that of grammatical-historical-rhetorical or the grammatical-historical-literary approach.[10]

The literary approach is reflective of developments outside of biblical studies, mainly in the area of literature and literary criticism. Largely from the field of literary criticism came what Carl F. H. Henry once referred to as the specter of postmodernism. This cultural turn, like that of modernism, clearly impacted and continues to impact biblical interpretation. Within evangelicalism there are those who look favorably upon postmodernism, while there are, as can be

---

[8]Grant R. Osborne, *The Hermeneutical Spiral: A Comprehensive Introduction to Biblical Interpretation* (Downers Grove, IL: IVP Academic, 2006).
[9]Anthony C. Thiselton, *The Two Horizons: New Testament Hermeneutics as Philosophical Description* (Grand Rapids, MI: Eerdmans, 1980).
[10]Tremper Longman III, *Literary Approaches to Biblical Interpretation*, reprinted in *Foundations of Contemporary Interpretation*, 102.

guessed, those who see it rife with pitfalls. Regardless, one thing can be said of postmodernism—it certainly has changed the discussion of interpretation. Before we leave the discussion of modernism and biblical interpretation, one more brief word is in order concerning the influence of modernism on biblical scholarship outside of evangelical or theologically conservative circles.

In a word, the influence of modernism has resulted in accommodation, the accommodation, that is, of the biblical text to the tenets of modernity. This can be clearly seen in the work of New Testament scholar Rudolf Bultmann. Bultmann is associated with the term *demythologizing*—not a word you see every day. Bultmann held the New Testament to be bound to the mythological world of the ancients, which makes the task of the interpreter that of finding "a truth that is independent of the mythical word picture," adding that it is "the task of theology to demythologize the Christian proclamation." Bultmann continues, "We cannot use electric lights and radios and, in the event of illness, avail ourselves of modern medical and clinical means and at the same time believe in the spirit and wonder world of the New Testament." The New Testament as it comes to us moderns, Bultmann argues, is an ancient book. We can't read it literally or take it literally because we live in the modern, not the ancient, world. We must accommodate the ancient text to our modern world.[11]

Bernard Ramm explains the dangers of this cultural accommodation that Bultmann represents: "The liberals asserted that the Scriptures were not only accommodated in form but also in matter of content."[12] Ramm provides the specific example of Christ's atonement. The cross meant one thing to the first century. Given cultural accommodation, the cross must mean something different for us. This is true of the resurrection of Christ, the birth of Christ, and so on down the line. Karl Barth, engaged in almost a lifelong corre-

---

[11]Rudolf Bultmann, "New Testament and Mythology: The Problem of Demythologizing the New Testament Proclamation," *New Testament Mythology and Other Basic Writings* (Philadelphia: Fortress Press, 1984), 2–5.
[12]Bernard Ramm, *Protestant Biblical Interpretation: A Textbook of Hermeneutics*, 3rd revised edition (Grand Rapids, MI: Baker, 1970), 101.

spondence and interaction with Bultmann, consistently critiqued his colleague for his cultural accommodation. The word of God stands over us, Barth told Bultmann, not the other way around.

Figure 5.1
Interpretation Timeline

1872–1873	Charles Hodge publishes "Rules of Interpretation."
1910–1913	James Orr publishes "Holy Scripture and Modern Negations."
1941	Rudolf Bultmann publishes "New Testament and Mythology."
1967	Jacques Derrida gives his "Structure, Sign, and Play" lecture on deconstruction.
1970	Bernard Ramm publishes *Protestant Biblical Interpretation*.
1970	Brevard S. Childs publishes *Biblical Theology in Crisis*.
1974	Hans Frei publishes *The Eclipse of Biblical Narrative*.
1977	Anthony C. Thiselton publishes "The New Hermeneutic."
1980	Walter C. Kaiser publishes "Legitimate Hermeneutics."
1980	Thiselton publishes *The Two Horizons*.
1982	ICBI members sign "The Chicago Statement on Biblical Hermeneutics."
1982	Bruce K. Waltke publishes "Historical Grammatical Problems."
1984	Earl Radmacher and Robert Preus publish *Hermeneutics, Inerrancy, and the Bible* by ICBI members.
1986	Donald K. McKim publishes *A Guide to Contemporary Hermeneutics*.
1986	D. A. Carson and John D. Woodbridge edit and publish *Hermeneutics, Authority, and Canon* by ICBI members.
1987	Tremper Longman publishes *Literary Approaches to Biblical Interpretation*.
1988	Harvie Conn edits and publishes *Inerrancy and Hermeneutic* by Westminster Seminary faculty.
1992	Thiselton publishes *New Horizons in Hermeneutics*.
1994	Donald G. Bloesch publishes *Holy Scripture*.
2005	Vanhoozer publishes "Lost in Interpretation" and *The Drama of Doctrine*.

"IT DEPENDS ON WHAT THE MEANING OF 'IS' IS": POSTMODERNISM AND THE CRISIS OF INTERPRETATION

While much can be and has been said of postmodernism and interpretation or meaning, for our purposes four points of discussion are worth bringing into sharp focus. The first concerns the field of epistemology and the extent to which we can know and the related question of the extent to which we can know from texts. The next three points are a bit more direct. The second point concerns the recovery of narrative or the focus on story or, perhaps more accurately, stories. Thirdly, there is the role of the community in reading and interpreting texts. Finally, there is the notion of humility in interpreting texts.

Of all places, Lewis Carroll's *Through the Looking Glass* might give us some insight into the postmodern challenge of meaning in texts. Consider this exchange between Humpty Dumpty and Alice. Carroll cleverly relays the dialogue: "'When I use a word,' Humpty Dumpty said, in a rather scornful tone, 'it means just what I choose it to mean, neither more nor less.'" Not quite ready to give in to Humpty Dumpty's argument, Alice counters, "The question is . . . whether you *can* make words mean so many different things." Undeterred, Humpty Dumpty returns, "'The question is . . . which is to be master—that's all.'" Then Carroll takes the whole thing one step further:

> Alice was too much puzzled to say anything; so after a minute Humpty Dumpty began again. "They've a temper, some of them— particularly verbs: they're the proudest—adjectives you can do anything with, but not verbs—however, *I* can manage the whole lot of them! Impenetrability! That's what *I* say!"
>
> "Would you tell me, please," said Alice, "what that means?"
>
> "Now you talk like a reasonable child," said Humpty Dumpty, looking very much pleased. "I meant by 'impenetrability' that we've had enough of that subject, and it would be just as well if you'd mention what you mean to do next, as I suppose you don't mean to stop here all the rest of your life."
>
> "That's a great deal to make one word mean," Alice said in a thoughtful tone.
>
> "When I make a word do a lot of work like that," said Humpty Dumpty, "I always pay it extra."

Carroll gives us a very clever and funny selection that is also rather philosophically engaging. What do words mean? Do they mean only what we want them to mean? Do we fill words with meaning? Is meaning arbitrary? And who decides? While the debate over meaning is carried on within a postmodern context, such a debate is not limited to the postmodern context. In the latter Middle Ages, a sharp debate arose between the nominalists and the realists. The realists claimed that language was absolute and that words represented what things truly were. The nominalists, on the other hand, made a case that words are arbitrary names (hence nominalism) that we ascribe to things. Out of this debate came the eternal question, enshrined by Shakespeare, "Is a rose by any other name still a rose?" The nominalist would answer with a resounding "Yes," while the realist would be equally convinced that the answer is a definite and unequivocal "No." Umberto Eco wrote his novel *The Name of the Rose* (1983), set in the 1300s, to show the connections of this age-old discussion to contemporary debates over words and meaning. Alice indeed raised a most philosophical question when she asked, "Would you tell me, please, what that means?" Or as a recent American President put it, what is the meaning of *is*?

To state this development more concretely, postmodernism has brought about a crisis in meaning. Or, perhaps more fairly, postmodernism draws attention to the empty meanings offered by modernism. An oft-repeated definition of postmodernism is that provided by Jean-François Lyotard. He observed, "I define postmodernism as incredulity towards metanarratives." Metanarratives are his way of expressing modernity's attempt to offer meaning. Metanarratives are stories (narratives) that stand over and above us (from the Greek preposition *meta*, meaning "over" or "above"). Like some grand arch, these metanarratives provide a grand story that we can tap into or connect with in order to find meaning. Lyotard is suspicious that any such metanarrative exists.

There is a bit of a debate between evangelicals over how to interpret Lyotard. Did Lyotard intend to include the biblical story as a metanarrative or did he not? James K. A. Smith and John Franke claim that the biblical story is excluded from Lyotard's denouncement. Others, such as J. P. Moreland and Millard Erickson, are, to use Lyotard's own term, incredulous at such a thought, seeing in Lyotard's definition the denouncement of Christianity and the Bible.

To these folks, the metanarratives that Lyotard writes off include the biblical one.[13]

Therein lies the difference among evangelical receptions of postmodernism. Some see it as a helpful defeater of modernity, helpful in that it challenges modernism as a worldview antithetical to Christianity. Others see postmodernism as itself antithetical to Christianity. The difference comes into sharper focus when the discussion turns to Jacques Derrida and the subject of deconstruction. Derrida is taken to mean, though interpreting him can be a challenge, that words and meaning are elusive. He rejects the views of the likes of E. D. Hirsch that the author's meaning can be discovered. Instead, Derrida finds meaning(s) in the hands of the readers. Closely related to deconstructionism is what has come to be called reader-response theory. As can be assumed from the title, the responsibility of meaning falls on the reader and the reader's experience of the text rather than on the author and the author's intended meaning. The opposite of objectivity and neutrality, the goals of modernity's scientific method, this approach celebrates subjectivity. The term that postmoderns prefer over subjectivity, however, is "situatedness," conveying the idea that texts and the interpreters of texts are situated in a given historical and cultural context that colors and influences how they see the world.

It should be abundantly clear that in these new waters of postmodernism, just as with modernism, danger lurks. It's probably a bit more of a complex problem, though, than wholesale rejection or acceptance. One thing that is worth mentioning in light of evangelicals' embrace of postmodernism is the irony of their critique of modernity. Those who embrace postmodernism do so because they argue that the work of biblical scholars and theologians was too bound up with modernity. From this new stance of postmodernism, the accommodation of modernity, including a naive appropriation of neutrality and objectivity, is quite clear to them. The irony is

---

[13]Jean-François Lyotard, *The Postmodern Condition: A Report on Knowledge* (Minneapolis: University of Minnesota Press, 1984), xxiv; James K. A. Smith, *Who's Afraid of Postmodernism?: Taking Derrida, Lyotard, and Foucault to Church* (Grand Rapids, MI: Baker, 2006).

that they very well may be too wedded to postmodernism. Cultural moods and movements tend not to be either/or, good or bad. Instead they tend to be a mixture. Wisdom and faithful discipleship require that we sort it all out rather than reflexively accept and reject. The work of Kevin Vanhoozer models well this more subtle and complex approach to the modernism/postmodernism divide as he rejects reactionary responses in favor of careful and critical engagement.[14]

Along those lines, it may be appropriate to ask if there is any positive gain from the postmodern development. This can be addressed by looking at the final three points concerning postmodernism: the recovery of narrative or stories, the role of community in interpretation, and the issue of epistemological and interpretive humility.

Hans Frei's book *The Eclipse of Biblical Narrative* (1974) launched a new movement, narrative theology. This movement is sometimes referred to as the "Yale School," where Frei taught.[15] Frei argued that both conservative and liberal approaches to the Bible, conditioned by modernity, attempted to locate meaning in the historical event, not in the text. Instead he looked to the text, the literary narrative, as the location of meaning. Because of his distance from the liberal position, this approach is sometimes called "postliberalism"—yet another *post*. But in the end the Yale School may suffer overreaction by not paying significant or even enough attention to the historicity of the text or the historicity of the events in the narrative. Cognizant of these problems, evangelicals of a more conservative stripe asked what good might be in narrative theology despite the bad. Again, the work of Kevin Vanhoozer is instructive.

Vanhoozer looks at this issue in terms of how we think about doctrine. He points to previous generations of evangelical theologians as understanding doctrine to mean propositional truth. He

---

[14]Kevin J. Vanhoozer, *Is There a Meaning in This Text? The Bible, the Reader, and the Morality of Literary Knowledge* (Grand Rapids, MI: Zondervan, 1998).
[15]Hans Frei, *The Eclipse of Biblical Narrative: A Study in Eighteenth and Nineteenth Century Hermeneutics* (New Haven, CT: Yale University Press, 1974).

names it the Hodge-Henry (or H-H) hypothesis, for Charles Hodge and Carl F. H. Henry. Vanhoozer does not wish to turn his back on propositions. On the contrary, he affirms that doctrine is "richly propositional." Vanhoozer just adds the "drama of redemption" to the mix, speaking of "theodramatic" doctrine.[16] This is a way of saying that the Bible itself is not reduced to propositions but is a narrative of the grand drama of redemption. But the Bible also contains propositional truth, facts. To a Philadelphia radio audience in the winter months of 1935, J. Gresham Machen observed, "Here is a rule for you my friends: no facts, no good news; no good news, no hope. The Bible is quite useless unless it is a record of facts." Then he added, "Thank God, it is a record of facts." Machen also expressed what this record of facts can do: "It will probe very deep into your life. It will reveal the dark secrets of your sin. But then it will bring you good tidings of salvation as no word of man can do."[17] Some theologians and biblical scholars have difficulty seeing both. But a hermeneutic that is sensitive to both may very well serve the church best.

Postmoderns, they tell us, enjoy stories, while moderns looked to "facts." To cite the old drama *Dragnet*, we're not interested in the story alone. "Just the facts, ma'am," says the modernist. The postmodern wants to hear the story, wants to go down the rabbit trails. The Bible has both facts (propositions) and stories. Consequently, a hermeneutic and even a homiletic that ignores either one will likely result in a lopsided theology, discipleship, and church. Postmodern evangelicals freely jettisoning propositions will likely live to regret it. Modern evangelicals who only wish to stick with the facts will likely do so too.

Postmodernism also stresses truth in community. Richard Rorty put this forth in his essay "Solidarity or Objectivity?"[18] Truth is

---

[16]Kevin J. Vanhoozer, "Lost in Interpretation," *Journal of the Evangelical Theological Society* 48:1 (March 2005), 89–114. See also his *The Drama of Doctrine: A Canonical-Linguistic Approach to Christian Theology* (Louisville: Westminster John Knox Press, 2005).

[17]J. Gresham Machen, "Do We Believe in Verbal Inspiration?" The radio addresses were published as *The Christian Faith in the Modern World* (New York: Macmillan, 1936), 57–58.

[18]Richard Rorty, *Objectivity, Relativism, and Truth*, Philosophical Papers, Vol. 1 (Cambridge: Cambridge University Press, 1991).

not a matter of objective facts, of absolutes, argues Rorty. Truth is a product of the group. If enough agree (solidarity), then that may count for truth. Rorty puts a twist on the saying that there is strength in numbers. In his view, there is truth in numbers. Truth or truths do not merely belong to communities; communities make or establish truth or truths. Consequently, things are true only within the group. This idea that truth is limited to its function within groups rather than functioning as true for all peoples in all times in all places has led to an emphasis on community and communities. Again, this can be good and bad. As for the bad, some limit the truth of Christianity as only truth within the Christian community, a practice that plays perfectly to pluralism. Such an approach should be rejected outright. The Christian story is not one story among stories; the Christian community is not one option among options. It is *the* story; it is *the* community. One positive impact of this development of community-based truth is the rise of the "theological interpretation" of the Scripture.

First, a caveat is in order. The theological interpretation is not necessarily bound to Rorty's epistemology or a community-based approach to truth. But what theological interpretation does pay attention to is the way the text is understood in communities, past and present. Rorty got it wrong when it comes to the basis of truth. But he might be right insofar as he draws attention to the way that the community, in its given time and place, shapes the way we see and interpret the world. This theological interpretation approach looks at how texts were understood and received in the past, the history of interpretation. It also does not distance the community from the text but rather acknowledges that communities shape texts, and texts shape communities. Or at least communities should be shaped by texts.

The work of Anthony Thiselton may be helpful to make this concrete and to point to the positive impact. He writes, "Doctrine may be perceived as the corporate memory and communal celebration of the narratives and drama of God's action in the world and in the life of Israel and the church." Then he adds, "These communities, even if separated in time and place, perceive themselves as taking their stand staking their identity through *sharing in the same narrative*, and through the recital and retelling of the same founding events." Thiselton suggests that hermeneutics and doctrine are in a symbiotic relationship, not two distinct disciplines quarantined off from each other. In this interplay of hermeneutics and doctrine, the church's task is to *remember* the narrative and to *retell* the narrative, and in the process we *participate* in the story, becoming the embodiment of Christ on earth, the Christian community, in our given place and time. Theological interpretation, in the end, brings together what had been previously put asunder, the wedding of hermeneutics and theology.[19]

One other danger deriving from postmodernism's emphasis on truth in community concerns the issue of situatedness. The claim is being made that not only is the interpreter "situated" in a context, but the biblical author is also "situated" in a context. While that is true to a certain extent, if taken to an extreme it can be gravely problematic. If the Bible is entirely culture-bound, then it offers no place for us to stand, no reference point beyond our experience. Israel's story, the Old Testament, is just that particular community's understanding and appropriation of God at the particular moment. As we read Israel's story, we simply accommodate it to our new cultural moment. This risks diminishing the biblical text, reducing it to a level on par with our take on the world. Curiously, this postmodern notion looks strangely like Bultmann's modernist demythologizing. It's one thing to acknowledge that the Bible was given in space and time, in a particular cultural context. It's quite another thing altogether to claim that the Bible is therefore culture-bound.

That leaves one last matter for discussion, humility in interpretation. A caricature of modernism has it that if you have the right method, applied correctly, you will arrive at the right interpreta-

---

[19]Anthony C. Thiselton, *The Hermeneutics of Doctrine* (Grand Rapids, MI: Eerdmans, 2007), 43–47. For more on theological interpretation, see *The Dictionary for Theological Interpretation of the Bible*, ed. Kevin J. Vanhoozer (Grand Rapids, MI: Baker, 2005).

tion. Science rules, and the scientific method is unassailable. This is the triumph of the lab coat. Think of television commercials for medicines. The actors wear lab coats, and to especially prove how reliable the product is, the commercials are set in laboratories with fascinating charts, equipment, and test tubes bubbling away. And people buy it, literally. It is, after all, science, and science can't be wrong. Sticking with the area of medicine may be instructive. Previous generations accepted the word of their family doctor or personal physician. These days one will check WebMD on their Blackberry while in the doctor's office. The idea that science is unassailable is passing; the tyranny of the lab coat is coming to an end. One upshot of this cultural shift concerning hermeneutics is the discussion of humility in interpretation. (Another is the whole question of pastoral authority, but that's definitely the subject of another book.) Physicians don't always get it right. And neither do interpreters of the Bible, even if they have the perfect hermeneutical method perfectly applied.

As with the other developments in postmodernism, caution is in order here too. Humility can translate into a paralyzing tentativeness in interpretation on the one hand, or it can lead to a radical democratization of interpretations on the other. The twilight of the tyranny of the lab coat can mean, dangerously, that expert opinions are entirely discarded. In the church this can be especially dangerous. The New Testament endorses the office of teacher, a God-given gift to the church. Teachers err and, worse, can abuse their role and power. But they still play a role in the church. Despite these pitfalls, it might be helpful to listen to the postmodern world and hear the desire to be humble in our understandings. There is truth, and there is our apprehension of the truth. Or to put the matter differently, there is the text, and then there is our interpretation of the text. As with the other points of our discussion of postmodernism, reactionary responses of wholesale acceptance or rejection of epistemological humility and interpretive humility likely won't help much in our desire to understand the text better and to live out the text in our world.

CONCLUSION, OR HOW TO READ THE BIBLE

In light of these descriptions of hermeneutics in both modern and postmodern contexts, it might be helpful to suggest something along the lines of prescription. In other words, beyond discussing how we read the Bible (description), we also need to think of how we *should* read the Bible (prescription). As a thumbnail sketch, we suggest reading the Bible reverently, prayerfully, collectively, humbly, carefully, Christologically, and obediently.

Remembering the Bible is the word of God, the revelation of the Creator and Redeemer, means above all reading the Bible *reverently*. The Bible is fascinating literature. The Bible is the subject of theological debate. The Bible is a challenging historical text. The Bible can be a puzzle, an enigma. The Bible can be a source of delight, of comfort. Above all, however, the Bible is the revealed word of the living God. Moderns had such difficulties with Scripture because it stood over them, requiring submission. The Bible stands over disciples as well, requiring submission of them too. Reading the Bible reverently means that to a certain extent we read the Bible as we read other texts, applying the rules of interpretation to it as we do to the other texts, but only to a certain extent. The Bible's difference from every other piece of literature, no matter how profound or how grand and eloquent that literature may be, demands our reverence.

Secondly, we need to read the Bible *prayerfully*. Near the end of John 13, Christ tells the disciples that he is about to leave them, news that floods them with anxiety (13:31–14:14). To comfort the disciples, Christ first informs them that they too will follow him eventually (14:3). He also comforts them by telling them of the gift of the Spirit. In John 14–16, Christ promises again and again to send the Spirit, the one who will lead them into all truth (14:16–18, 25–26; 15:26–27; 16:7–15).[20] By extension this promise of the Spirit extends to disciples today, to us. We have the Spirit to guide us into truth.

Reading the Bible reverently and prayerfully runs counter to

---

[20]For a full discussion of these texts, see D. A. Carson, *The Gospel According to John: The Pillar New Testament Commentary* (Grand Rapids: Eerdmans, 2000).

prevailing notions of modernism. Reading the Bible solely or merely as an individual plays into the notions of modernism. Reading the Bible *collectively* is a good antidote to such privatized, individual reading. In his classic text on discipleship as community, *Life Together*, Dietrich Bonhoeffer spoke convincingly of reading the Bible collectively, though he also was careful to stress the need for private, devotional reading as well. Reading the Bible collectively eventually puts us, Bonhoeffer observes, within the community of the text. He writes, "We become a part of what once took place for our salvation. Forgetting and losing ourselves, we, too, pass through the Red Sea, through the desert, across the Jordan into the promised land. . . . We are torn out of our own existence and set down in the midst of holy history."[21] Reading the Bible collectively also puts us in the historical and global community, which means that the Bible is not our individual possession. Rather, the Bible is the book of the body of Christ. That body of Christ extends back in time and around the globe. Asking how historical and other cultural communities read the text not only can be a fruitful exercise, it is evidence that we truly believe that the body of Christ is bigger than we are.

This can be especially tricky for contemporary American evangelicals, who tend to look down on the past and tradition ("newer is better") and who tend to assume the role of "teacher" to the rest of the world, not that of fellow disciple and learner. Looking at the history of interpretation and listening to the interpretations of others across the globe can save us from blind spots and missteps in our reading of the text. C. S. Lewis once commended the practice of reading something old every time he read something new or current. In addition to taking his advice, we should also consider reading something from outside our particular cultural context as well as books by people who look like we do. Consider, for instance, reading the recently published *African Bible Commentary* alongside western commentaries.[22]

---

[21]Dietrich Bonhoeffer, *Life Together*, trans. John W. Doberstein (New York: Harper & Row, 1954), 53.

[22]Tokunboh Adeyemo, general editor, *African Bible Commentary: A One-Volume Commentary Written by 70 African Scholars* (Grand Rapids, MI: Zondervan, 2006).

This leads to the next step, reading the Bible *humbly*. Postmodernism has introduced the notion of epistemological humility. This, of course, carries with it the potential to run astray. There needs to be a place to land. Leaving meaning and interpretation up in the air, as always tentative, can cause significant problems for theology and church practice and worship. But there is also the danger in the other direction, namely, being too sure about one's interpretation. It's helpful to read the Bible humbly, to be careful not to equate our interpretations of the text with the text itself. The Bible is inerrant, in other words, but our interpretations are not. Even if we have the right hermeneutical method and apply it perfectly, we still may get it wrong. This is a bit of walking a tightrope, but reading the Bible humbly can go a long way.

We also need to read the Bible *carefully*, which is to say there is a place for hermeneutic and rules of interpretation. Over the past century and a half or so, there has been a growing consensus that a proper hermeneutic consists of the historical-grammatical-cultural-rhetorical (or literary) method. Reading the Bible carefully also entails reading the Bible canonically. In previous ages of the church, this was referred to as the "analogy of faith," which amounted to reading particular texts of the Bible in light of the whole Bible. In very practical terms, this means we can't read the Old Testament as if the New Testament didn't exist. We can take a canonical reading one step further and call it a Christological reading. Also in very practical terms, this means we can't read any part of the Bible, Old or New Testament books, as if the passage at hand had no connection to Christ.

We need to read the Bible *Christologically*. The Bible is ultimately the story of Christ. All of it points to or away from him, like spokes from the hub of the wheel. All of the Bible eventually finds its end, its design, its purpose in Christ. Theologians and biblical scholars refer to this as a *Christotelic* reading of the Bible. The *telic* part comes from the Greek word *telos*, meaning "end" or "purpose." It's not too much of a stretch to say that we understand a text fully when we connect it to Christ and his mission.

Finally, we need to read the Bible *obediently*. Reading and interpreting are first-order activities that lead to the second-order activity of obedience and practice (James 2:22–27). Reading and interpreting the Bible is actually the easy part, compared to taking the Bible seriously enough to act upon it. God's word stands above us, and even above our cultural assumptions about the world. Obedient disciples not only hear the word above the noise and static and distortion, they do it.

Both modernism and postmodernism have their downside and their upside, as tends to be the case with most cultural developments. The development and practice of hermeneutics in the modern age has helpfully pointed the church to reading the Bible carefully, to applying the rules of interpretation. Postmodernism, despite having many potential pitfalls, has also helpfully reminded the church to read the Bible collectively and humbly. Reading the Bible reverently, prayerfully, collectively, humbly, carefully, and obediently comes with no guarantees that we will get it right. Hermeneutics, after all, claims to be both a science and an art. Any artist will tell you that there is technique (science) involved, but there is also skill (art). The former can be taught and studied. The latter comes over time and with maturity.

Whether we live in a modern, ultramodern, or postmodern age, one thing remains certain: we need something beyond ourselves and beyond our experience to make sense of it all. We need meaning. The ancient book of Scripture provided meaning for ancient people, but it also provides meaning for moderns, ultramoderns, and even postmoderns. On that we can rest. That's what makes the word of God, this ancient book, the good news for all peoples in all ages.

> "All flesh is like grass
>> and all its glory is like the flower of grass.
>> The grass withers,
>> and the flower falls,
>> but the word of the Lord remains forever."
> And this word is the good news that was preached to you.
> (1 Peter 1:24–25)

6

Among the three elements of the doctrine of Scripture considered in this book, the interpretation of the Bible has received the most consideration in all theological quarters. The discussion and disagreement over the principles that should guide accurate interpretation have arisen over opposing suppositions about the nature and composition of Scripture, differences in the focus of interpretation (author, text, audience), and shifts in philosophical understandings of truth and meaning. At the same time, some principles have remained surprisingly consistent. This chapter covers some of the most significant positions and transitions from several leading voices from the early days to the close of the modern age.[1]

SOURCES ON INTERPRETATION

These are listed in the order of quotation in this chapter.

Charles Hodge, *Systematic Theology*, Vol. 1, "Rules of Interpretation."

Walter C. Kaiser Jr., "Legitimate Hermeneutics."

Vern S. Poythress, *God-Centered Biblical Interpretation*.

Tremper Longman III, *Literary Approaches to Biblical Interpretation*.

Bernard Ramm, *Protestant Biblical Interpretation*.

Rudolf Bultmann, "New Testament and Mythology."

---

[1]An excellent introduction to scholarly evangelical contribution to the field of interpretation is David Alan Black and David S. Dockery, eds., *New Testament Criticism and Interpretation* (Grand Rapids, MI: Zondervan, 1991).

Brevard S. Childs, *Biblical Theology in Crisis.*
Hans W. Frei, *The Eclipse of Biblical Narrative.*
Anthony C. Thiselton, "The New Hermeneutic."
James Orr, "Holy Scripture and Modern Negations."
Bruce K. Waltke, "Historical Grammatical Problems."

UNDERSTANDING INTERPRETATION

Among theological conservatives in the modern age, assumptions about the proper interpretation of the Bible have remained fairly constant. The basic tenets include the clarity (or perspicuity) of Scripture, the right and responsibility of the believer to understand God's word, and the ability of the individual to seek out its meaning. The following excerpts by noted conservative theologians Charles Hodge and Walter Kaiser, divided by more than one hundred years, share the conviction that interpreting the Bible is at root a straightforward task. At the same time the passages convey an increase in the awareness of interpretive complexities from Hodge's day to Kaiser's.

Charles Hodge, "Rules of Interpretation" (1872–1873)

If every man has the right, and is bound to read the Scriptures, and to judge for himself what they teach, he must have certain rules to guide him in the exercise of this privilege and duty. These rules are not arbitrary. They are not imposed by human authority. They have no binding force which does not flow from their own intrinsic truth and propriety. They are few and simple.

1. The words of Scripture are to be taken in their plain historical sense. That is, they must be taken in the sense attached to them in the age and by the people to whom they were addressed. This only assumes that the sacred writers were honest, and meant to be understood.

2. If the Scriptures be what they claim to be, the word of God, they are the work of one mind, and that mind divine. From this it follows that Scripture cannot contradict Scripture. God cannot teach in one place anything which is inconsistent with what he

teaches in another. Hence Scripture must explain Scripture. If a passage admits of different interpretations, that only can be the true one which agrees with what the Bible teaches elsewhere on the same subject. If the Scriptures teach that the Son is the same in substance and equal in power and glory with the Father, then when the Son says, "The Father is greater than I," the superiority must be understood in a manner consistent with this equality. It must refer either to subordination as to the mode of subsistence and operation, or it must be official. A king's son may say, "My father is greater than I," although personally his father's equal. This rule of interpretation is sometimes called the analogy of Scripture, and sometimes the analogy of faith. There is no material difference in the meaning of the two expressions.

3. The Scriptures are to be interpreted under the guidance of the Holy Spirit, which guidance is to be humbly and earnestly sought. The ground of this rule is twofold: First, the Spirit is promised as a guide and teacher. He was to come to lead the people of God into the knowledge of the truth. And secondly, the Scriptures teach, that "the natural man receiveth not the things of the Spirit of God: for they are foolishness unto him; neither can he know them, because they are spiritually discerned" (1 Cor. 2:14). The unrenewed mind is naturally blind to spiritual truth. His heart is in opposition to the things of God. Congeniality of mind is necessary to the proper apprehension of divine things. As only those who have a moral nature can discern moral truth, so those only who are spiritually minded can truly receive the things of the Spirit.

The fact that all the true people of God in every age and in every part of the church, in the exercise of their private judgment, in accordance with the simple rules above stated, agree as to the meaning of Scripture in all things necessary either in faith or practice, is a decisive proof of the perspicuity of the Bible, and of the safety of allowing the people the enjoyment of the divine right of private judgment.[2]

---

[2]Charles Hodge, *Systematic Theology*, 3 vols. (Grand Rapids, MI: Eerdmans), 1:187–188.

Walter C. Kaiser Jr., "Legitimate Hermeneutics" (1980)

[M]an's basic ability to interpret is not derived from some science, technical skill, or exotic course open only to the more gifted intellects of society. The general principles of interpreting are not learned, invented, or discovered by people. They are part and parcel of the nature of man as a being made in the image of God. Given the gift of communication and speech itself, man already began to practice the principles of hermeneutics. The art has been in use from the moment God spoke to Adam in the Garden, and from the time Adam addressed Eve, until the present. In human conversation, the speaker is always the author; the person spoken to is always the interpreter. Correct understanding must always begin with the meanings the speaker attaches to his own words.

It is agreed that proper interpretation is more than a native art. The science of hermeneutics collects these observed rules as already practiced by native speakers and arranges them in an orderly way for the purpose of study and reflection. But such a science does not alter the fact that the rules were in operation before they were codified and examined. The situation here is exactly as it is with grammars and dictionaries: they do not prescribe what a language must do; they only describe how its best speakers and writers use it. So it is with hermeneutics.[3]

GRAMMATICAL-HISTORICAL INTERPRETATION

The principal approach to interpreting Scripture in conservative orthodox Christianity has long been that of the grammatical-historical.[4] In the following segment, Vern Poythress of Westminster Seminary in Philadelphia defends a "total engagement" view of the approach in which interpretation coincides with the reader's own spiritual transformation.

---

[3]Walter C. Kaiser Jr., "Legitimate Hermeneutics," in *A Guide to Contemporary Hermeneutics: Major Trends in Biblical Interpretation*, ed. Donald K. McKim (Grand Rapids, MI: Eerdmans, 1986), 114–115.
[4]There are several variations of the term, including historico-grammatical and grammatico-historical, all of which refer to the same basic interpretive approach.

Vern S. Poythress, God-Centered Biblical Interpretation (1999)

Interpretation of the Bible involves both a linguistic side, focusing on the language of the Bible, and a historical side, focusing on the events and the contexts in which they occur. As the once-for-all perspective reminds us, the authority and holiness of God demand that we pay attention to the original context of God's speech, in both its linguistic and its historical aspects. Thus, we may speak of *grammatical-historical* interpretation. Grammatical-historical interpretation focuses on the original context. But . . . its reflections cohere with the later transmission, the modern reception, and the significance of events in the total plan of God. Thus, grammatical-historical interpretation, rightly understood, is a perspective on a total engagement with God. It is a total process that interacts with everything that we know about God and includes our transformation into the image of Christ (2 Cor. 3:18). The grammatical aspect of the original context coheres with the speaking of God throughout history. The historical aspect of the original context coheres with the action of God and the plan of God throughout history. And our understanding of both aspects undergoes progressive transformation in our own individual and corporate history in the church today.[5]

THE AUTHOR'S INTENT IN COMMUNICATION

In conjunction with the grammatical-historical approach, several conservative biblical scholars emphasize the importance of studying and interpreting the Bible as a literary communication. In his book *Literary Approaches to Biblical Interpretation*, Tremper Longman, then professor of Old Testament at Westminster Seminary in Philadelphia, argued that meaningful communication involves the author, the text, and the reader. The excerpt below focuses on the importance of the author's intended meaning in interpretation and the human and divine dimensions of authorship.[6]

---

[5]Vern S. Poythress, *God-Centered Biblical Interpretation* (Phillipsburg, NJ: P&R, 1999), 164.
[6]A classic defense of authorial intent as the basis for meaning is literary critic E. D. Hirsch's book *Validity in Interpretation* (New Haven, CT: Yale, 1967).

Tremper Longman III, Literary Approaches to Biblical
Interpretation (1987)

If literature is an act of communication, then meaning resides
in the intention of the author. The author encoded a message for
the readers. Interpretation then has as its goal the recovery of the
author's purpose in writing. . . . The hypothetical and probable
nature of interpretation enters the picture because we cannot read
minds and thus cannot be absolutely certain that we have recovered
the correct meaning of a text. This fact should not lead us to throw
up our hands in despair. . . . The view that the author is the locus of
the meaning of a text provides theoretical stability to interpretation.
Our interpretation is correct insofar as it conforms to the meaning
intended by the author. . . .

[An] issue concerning the intention of the author is the relationship between the human author and the divine author. God is
the ultimate author of the Scriptures, so it must be said that final
meaning resides in his intention. Of course, he condescended to
reveal his message to the biblical authors, who did not write in a
trance but had conscious intentions of their own. But it is wrong to
equate fully the intention of God with that of the human author. For
instance, the application in the New Testament of an Old Testament
text frequently exceeds the obvious meaning intended by the author
of the latter.[7]

ACCOMMODATION

The topic of God's accommodation to human individuals has
appeared repeatedly in this book, as it has in the discussion of the
doctrine of Scripture throughout the modern age. In the following
passage, theologian and professor Bernard Ramm explains accommodation within the framework of interpretation.

---

[7]Tremper Longman III, *Literary Approaches to Biblical Interpretation*, in *Foundations of
Contemporary Interpretation*, ed. Moisés Silva (Grand Rapids, MI: Zondervan, 1996), 135. For
more on literary forms in the Bible, see Kevin J. Vanhoozer, "The Semantics of Biblical Literature:
Truth and Scripture's Diverse Literary Forms," in *Hermeneutics, Authority, and Canon*, ed. D. A.
Carson and John D. Woodbridge (Grand Rapids, MI: Zondervan, 1986), 49–104.

Bernard Ramm, Protestant Biblical Interpretation (1970)

Holy Scripture is the truth of God accommodated to the human mind so that the human mind can assimilate it. The Scriptures were written in three known languages of man (Hebrew, Aramaic, Greek). The Scriptures were written in a human or social environment and its analogies are drawn from that environment. When we learn the content of that environment we can know the meaning of the revealed analogy.

Through such accommodation the truth of God can get through to man and be a meaningful revelation. Stated another way, revelation must have an anthropomorphic character.

The accommodated character of divine revelation is especially obvious in such instances as the tabernacle and in the parabolic teaching of Christ. In both instances the human and earthly vehicle is the bearer of spiritual truth. Our understanding of the spiritual world is *analogous*. . . . The fact of God's almightiness is spoken of in terms of a right arm because among men the right arm is the symbol of strength or power. Pre-eminence is spoken of as sitting at God's right hand because in human social affairs the right hand position with reference to the host was the place of greatest honor. . . .

This anthropomorphic character of Scripture is nothing against Scripture, but it is necessary for the communication of God's truth to man. This the interpreter will always keep in mind. . . .

The interpreter who is aware of this anthropomorphic character of the divine revelation will not be guilty of grotesque forms of literal exegesis. More than one unlettered person and cultist has taken the anthropomorphisms of the Scriptures literally and has so thought of God as possessing a body.

Before leaving this subject of accommodation of Scripture it is necessary to declare our rejection of the liberals' use of the idea of accommodation. . . . To liberalism accommodation was the evisceration or enervation of the doctrinal content of the Bible by explaining doctrinal passages as accommodations to the thought-patterns of the times of the biblical writers. . . . Thus the liberals asserted that the Scriptures were not only accommodated in form but also in matter or content. This same sort of error is true in the *nth* degree in Bultmann's theory of the mythology of the New Testament. The atonement as a vicarious sacrifice is a way in which first-century Christians thought of the cross but, it is asserted, we are not bound today to think of the cross in that manner.[8]

MYTHOLOGICAL WORLD PICTURE

Within the realm of higher-critical approaches, Rudolf Bultmann focused on the existential interpretation of the Bible, or how a modern individual might understand and "relive" the message of Christianity.[9] But as a modern person, Bultmann would not accept as scientifically and historically truthful what he called the mythology in the New Testament. In the excerpt below, he discusses how demythologizing is central to interpretation that speaks to the modern person.

Rudolf Bultmann, "New Testament and Mythology" (1941)

All of this [the world picture of the New Testament and salvation history] is mythological talk, and the individual motifs may be easily traced to the contemporary mythology of Jewish apocalypticism and of the Gnostic myth of redemption. Insofar as it is mythological talk it is incredible to men and women today because for them the mythical world picture is a thing of the past. Therefore, contemporary Christian proclamation is faced with the question whether, when it demands faith from men and women, it expects them to acknowledge the mythical world picture of the past. If this is impossible, it then has to face the question whether the New Testament proclamation has a truth that is independent of the mythical world picture, in which case it would be the task of theology to demythologize the Christian proclamation.

No mature person represents God as a being who exists above

---

[8]Bernard Ramm, *Protestant Biblical Interpretation: A Textbook of Hermeneutics*, 3rd rev. ed. (Grand Rapids, MI: Baker, 1970), 99–101.
[9]Bultmann limits his discussion to the New Testament when he speaks of the Christian proclamation because he rejected the Old Testament as part of the Christian Scripture.

in heaven; in fact, for us there no longer is any "heaven" in the old sense of the word. And just as certainly there is no hell, in the sense of a mythical underworld beneath the ground on which we stand. Thus, the stories of Christ's descent and ascent are finished, and so is the expectation of the Son of man's coming on the clouds of heaven and of the faithful's being caught up to meet him in the air (1 Thess. 4:15ff).

We cannot use electric lights and radios and, in the event of illness, avail ourselves of modern medical and clinical means and at the same time believe in the spirit and wonder world of the New Testament. And if we suppose that we can do so ourselves, we must be clear that we can represent this as the attitude of Christian faith only by making the Christian proclamation unintelligible and impossible for our contemporaries.[10]

THE CANONICAL APPROACH

Like Bultmann, proponents of the canonical approach saw the need for the Bible, as the word of God, to speak to modern individuals. In stark contrast to him, however, the canonical interpreters did not see Scripture as a book of only loosely related documents to be separated and edited in accordance with the latest scientific and rational convictions. Rather, they believed that the Bible is to be interpreted and understood as a unified whole—in light of both Testaments, all literary genres, and all degrees of scientific and historical accuracy. Not all its contents are necessarily true, so these interpreters say, but they all function together. Brevard Childs, one of the foremost advocates of this approach, explains in the following segment how biblical interpretation (and biblical theology) must be done with respect to the canon and its context.

Brevard S. Childs, Biblical Theology in Crisis (1970)

[W]e would like to defend the thesis that the canon of the Christian church is the most appropriate context from which to

---

[10]Rudolf Bultmann, "New Testament and Mythology: The Problem of Demythologizing the New Testament Proclamation," *New Testament and Mythology and Other Basic Writings*, trans. and ed. Schubert M. Ogden (Philadelphia: Fortress, 1984), 2–5.

do biblical theology. What does this mean? First of all, implied in the thesis is the basic Christian confession, shared by all branches of historic Christianity, that the Old and New Testaments together constitute sacred Scripture for the Christian church. . . . The fundamental theological issue at stake is not the extent of the canon, which has remained in some flux within Christianity, but the claim for a normative body of tradition contained in a set of books.

Again, to speak of the canon as a context implies that these Scriptures must be interpreted in relation to their function within the community of faith that treasured them. The Scriptures of the church are not archives of the past but a channel of life for the continuing church, through which God instructs and admonishes his people. Implied in the use of the canon as a context for interpreting Scripture is a rejection of the method that would imprison the Bible within a context of the historical past. Rather, the appeal to the canon understands Scripture as a vehicle of a divine reality, which indeed encountered an ancient people in the historical past, but which continues to confront the church through the pages of Scripture. The church's prayer for illumination by the Holy Spirit when interpreting Scripture is no meaningless vestige from a forgotten age of piety, but an acknowledgment of the continuing need for God to make himself known through Scripture to an expectant people. Because the church uses the text as a medium of revelation the interrelation of Bible and theology is constitutive in the context of the canon. The descriptive and constructive aspects of interpretation may well be distinguished, but never separated when doing biblical theology according to this model.

To do biblical theology within the context of the canon involves acknowledgment of the *normative* quality of the biblical tradition. The Scriptures of the church provide the authoritative and definitive word that continues to shape and enliven the church. . . . If the word of God is to be anything, it must speak to a concrete situation in the present.[11]

---

[11]Brevard S. Childs, *Biblical Theology in Crisis* (Philadelphia: Westminster, 1970), 99–100.

BIBLICAL NARRATIVE INTERPRETATION

By the mid- to late-twentieth century, conservative and non-conservative scholars alike in the field of biblical interpretation were addressing the inadequacies of the higher-critical approaches. The vanguard of one non-conservative alternative, the "narrative theology" movement, came from the Divinity School at Yale University.[12] Attention to the narrative nature of the Bible became, for this approach, a means of understanding the meaning and function of Scripture and explaining biblical phenomena. In the following excerpt Hans Frei discusses the importance of narrative interpretation and why it is vital to understanding the realism of the biblical accounts. He uses the Synoptic Gospels as an example.

Hans W. Frei, The Eclipse of Biblical Narrative (1974)

By speaking of the narrative shape of these accounts [the Synoptic Gospels], I suggest that what they are about and how they make sense are functions of the depiction or narrative rendering of the events constituting them—including their being rendered, at least partially, by the device of chronological sequence. The claim, for example, that the gospel story is about Jesus of Nazareth as the Messiah means that it narrates the way his status came to be enacted. There are, of course, other kinds of stories that merely illustrate something we already know; and there are other stories yet that function in such a way as to express or conjure up an insight or an affective state that is beyond any and all depiction so that stories, though inadequate, are best fitted for the purpose because they are evocations, if not invocations, of a common archetypal consciousness or a common faith. In both of these latter cases the particular rendering is not indispensable, though it may be helpful to the point being made. Part of what I want to suggest is that the hermeneutical option espied but not really examined and thus cast aside in the

---

[12]The similar (though by no means identical) interpretive methods of George Lindbeck, Hans Frei, David Kelsey, and others at Yale Divinity School also resulted in this movement gaining the name "Yale School."

eighteenth and nineteenth centuries[13] was that many biblical narratives, especially the Synoptic Gospels, may belong to the first kind, for which their narrative rendering, in effect a cumulative account of the theme, is indispensable.

This is one of the chief characteristics of a narrative that is "realistic." In that term I include more than the indispensability of the narrative shape, including chronological sequence, to the meaning, theme, or subject matter of the story. The term realistic I take also to imply that the narrative depiction is of that particular sort in which characters or individual persons, in their internal depth or subjectivity as well as in their capacity as doers and sufferers of actions or events, are firmly and significantly set in the context of the external environment, natural but more particularly social. Realistic narrative is that mind in which subject and social setting belong together, and characters and external circumstances fitly render each other. Neither character nor circumstance separately, nor yet their interaction, is a shadow of something else more real or more significant. Nor is the one more important than the other in the story. . . .

In all these respects—inseparability of subject matter from its depiction or cumulative rendering, literal rather than symbolic quality of the human subject and his social context, mutual rendering of character, circumstance, and their interaction—a realistic narrative is like a historical account. This, of course, does not preclude differences between the two kinds of account. For example, it is taken for granted that modern historians will look with a jaundiced eye on appeal to miracle as an explanatory account of events. Historical accounting, by almost universal modern consent, involves that the narrative satisfactorily rendering a sequence believed to have taken place must consist of events, and reasons for their occurrence, whose connections may be rendered without recourse to supernatural agency. By contrast in the bibli-

---

[13]The purpose of Frei's book was to recount the disappearance of narrative interpretation in the eighteenth and nineteenth centuries in the wake of higher criticism, which he took to be detrimental to interpreting the Bible.

cal stories, of course, nonmiraculous and miraculous accounts and explanations are constantly intermingled. But in accordance with our definition, even the miraculous accounts are realistic or history-like (but not therefore historical and in that sense factually true) if they do not in effect symbolize something else instead of the action portrayed. That is to say, even such miraculous accounts are history-like or realistic if the depicted action is indispensable to the rendering of a particular character, divine or human, or a particular story. (And, in fact, biblical miracles are frequently and strikingly nonsymbolic.)

Finally, realistic narrative, if it is really seriously undertaken and not merely a pleasurable or hortatory exercise, is a sort in which in style as well as in content in the setting forth of didactic material, and in the depiction of characters and action, the sublime or at least serious effect mingles inextricably with the quality of what is casual, random, ordinary, and everyday. The intercourse and destinies of ordinary and credible individuals rather than stylized or mythical hero figures, flawed or otherwise, are rendered in realistic narratives. Furthermore, they are usually rendered in ordinary language. . . . Style and account go together: for example, the parabolic mode of Jesus's teaching integrates extraordinary themes with analogies drawn from workaday occurrences; and it does so in pithy, ordinary talk. Action and passion in realistic narrative illustrate the same principle. Believable individuals and their credible destinies are rendered in ordinary language and through concatenations of ordinary events which cumulatively constitute the serious, sublime, and even tragic impact of powerful historical forces. These forces in turn allow the ordinary, "random," lifelike individual persons, who become their bearers in the crucial intersection of character and particular event-laden circumstance, to become recognizable realistic "types," without thereby inducing a loss of their distinctively contingent or random individuality.[14]

---

[14]Hans W. Frei, *The Eclipse of Biblical Narrative: A Study of Eighteenth and Nineteenth Century Hermeneutics* (New Haven, CT: Yale, 1974), 13–15.

THE NEW HERMENEUTIC

Another significant approach to interpretation that rose to prominence in the twentieth century was "the new hermeneutic." Like the two previous methods in this chapter, the new hermeneutic stressed the importance of finding Scripture's fresh and relevant message for a modern time. In the following excerpt Anthony Thiselton, professor of Christian theology at the University of Nottingham, develops his view of the new hermeneutic in light of his understanding of Ernst Fuchs and Gerhard Ebeling,[15] two eminent twentieth-century German theologians.[16] The new hermeneutical method that Thiselton defends, with its emphasis on the interpreter and the translated word, serves as an excellent example of the philosophical and theological shift in the last quarter of the twentieth century from modernity to postmodernity.

Anthony C. Thiselton, "The New Hermeneutic" (1977)

The approach to the New Testament which has come to be known as the new hermeneutic is associated most closely with the work of Ernst Fuchs and Gerhard Ebeling. Both of these writers insist on its practical relevance to the world of today. How does language, especially the language of the Bible, strike home . . . to the modern hearer? How may its words so reach through into his own understanding that when he repeats them they will be *his* words? How may the word of God become a living word which is heard anew?

This emphasis on present application rather than simply antiquarian biblical research stems partly from connections between the new hermeneutic and the thought of Rudolf Bultmann, but also from a pastor's deep and consistent concern on the part of Fuchs and Ebeling, both of whom served as pastors for some

---

[15]Both Fuchs and Ebeling were students of Rudolf Bultmann. The existentialism of Bultmann's theology is strongly evident in Fuchs and Ebeling, as well as in Thiselton.

[16]In the years following the publication of this essay, Thiselton developed his presentation of the new hermeneutic in *The Two Horizons: New Testament Hermeneutics and Philosophical Description* (Grand Rapids, MI/London: Eerdmans/Paternoster, 1980) and in his general work on hermeneutics, *New Horizons in Hermeneutics* (Grand Rapids, MI: Zondervan, 1992).

years, about the relevance and effectiveness of Christian preaching. Central to Fuchs's work is the question "What do we have to do at our desks, if we want later to set the text in front of us in the pulpit?"[17]

It would be a mistake to conclude that this interest in preaching, however, is narrowly ecclesiastical or merely homiletical. Both writers share an intense concern about the position of the unbeliever. If the word of God is capable of *creating* faith, its intelligibility cannot be said to *presuppose* faith. Thus Fuchs warns us, "the proclamation loses its character when it anticipates (i.e. presupposes) confession,"[18] while Ebeling boldly asserts, "the criterion of the understandability of our preaching is not the believer but the nonbeliever. For the proclaimed word seeks to effect faith, but does not presuppose faith as a necessary preliminary. . . ."[19]

The key question in the new hermeneutic, then, is how the New Testament may speak to us *anew*. A literalistic repetition of the text cannot *guarantee* that it will "speak" to the modern hearer. He may understand all of its individual words, and yet fail to understand what is being said. In Wolfhart Pannenberg's words, "in a changed situation the traditional phrases, even when recited literally, do not mean what they did at the time of their original formulation."[20] Thus Ebeling asserts, "the *same word* can be said to another time only by being said differently."[21]

In assessing the validity of this point, we may well wish to make some proviso about the uniquely normative significance of the original formulation in *theology*. The problem is recognized by Fuchs and Ebeling perhaps more clearly than by Bultmann when parallel questions arise in his program of demythologizing. It is partly in connection with this problem that both writers insist on the necessity of historical-critical research on the New Testament. At the same time, at least two considerations reinforce their conten-

---

[17]Ernst Fuchs, *Studies of the Historical Jesus* (London: SCM, 1970), 8.
[18]Ibid., 30.
[19]Gerhard Ebeling, *Word and Faith* (Philadelphia: Fortress, 1963), 125.
[20]Wolfhart Pannenberg, *Basic Questions in Theology*, 2 vols. (London: SCM, 1970), 1:9.
[21]Gerhard Ebeling, "Time and Word," *The Future of Our Religious Past: Essays in Honour of Rudolf Bultmann*, ed. James M. Robinson (London: SCM, 1971), 265. Emphasis added.

tions about the inadequacy of mere repetition of the text from the standpoint of *hermeneutics*. First, we already recognize the fact that in translation from one language to another, literalism can be the enemy of faithful communication. "To put it into another language means to think it through afresh."[22] Second, we already have given tacit recognition to this principle whenever we stress the importance of preaching. The preacher "translates" the text by placing it at the point of encounter with the hearer, from which it speaks anew into his own world in his own language. But this hermeneutical procedure is demanded in *all* interpretation which is faithful to the New Testament. . . .[23]

QUESTIONING MODERN ASSUMPTIONS

Accomplished and respected scholars have long voiced their concerns about the direction in which modern—and now postmodern—interpretive methods are taking biblical studies. The passages below are authored by James Orr, the Scottish Presbyterian minister and professor of theology, and Bruce Waltke, professor of Old Testament and Hebrew. Orr encourages critical study of the Bible but urges caution as he responds to some of the presuppositions of the higher critics. Waltke, writing on the new hermeneutic, admits that there are things to be learned from the method but finds the inherent erosion of the objectivity of God's word to be detrimental. Both theologians are distressed by where modern (and early postmodern) interpretation is going and what it is doing to the Bible's authority.

James Orr, "Holy Scripture and Modern Negations" (c. 1910–1915)

By all means, let criticism have its rights. Let purely literary questions about the Bible receive full and fair discussion. Let the structure of books be impartially examined. If a reverent science has light to throw on the composition or authority or age of these

---

[22]Gerhard Ebeling, *The Nature of Faith* (London: SCM, 1961), 188.
[23]Anthony C. Thiselton, "The New Hermeneutic," in *A Guide to Contemporary Hermeneutics,* ed. Donald K. McKim (Grand Rapids, MI: Eerdmans, 1986), 78–81.

books, let its voice be heard. If this thing is of God we cannot overthrow it; if it be of man, or so far as it is of man, or so far as it comes in conflict with the reality of things in the Bible, it will come to naught—as in my opinion a great deal of it is fast coming today through its own excesses. No fright, therefore, need be taken at the mere word "criticism."

On the other hand, we are not bound to accept every wild critical theory that any critic may choose to put forward and assert, as the final word on the matter. We are entitled, nay, we are bound, to look at the presuppositions on which each criticism proceeds, and to ask, How far is the criticism controlled by those presuppositions? We are bound to look at the evidence by which the theory is supported, and to ask, Is it really borne out by the evidence? And when theories are put forward with every confidence as fixed results, and we find them, as we observe them, still in constant process of evolution and change, constantly becoming more complicated, more extreme, more fanciful, we are entitled to inquire, Is this the certainty that it was alleged to be? *Now that is my complaint against much of the current criticism of the Bible*—not that it is criticism, but that it starts from the wrong basis, that it proceeds by arbitrary methods, and that it arrives at results which I think are demonstrably false results. . . .

The process of thought in regard to Scripture is easily traced. First, there is an ostentatious throwing overboard, joined with some expression of contempt, of what is called the verbal inspiration of Scripture—a very much-abused term.[24] Jesus is still spoken of as the highest revealer, and it is allowed that his words, if only we could get at them—and on the whole it is thought we can—furnish the highest rule of guidance for time and for eternity. But even criticism, we are told, must have its rights. Even in the New Testament the Gospels go into the crucible, and in the name of synoptic criticism, historical criticism, they are subject to wonderful processes, in the course of which much of the history gets melted out or is peeled

---

[24]Interestingly, Orr did not personally adhere to verbal inspiration or inerrancy in the traditional sense that Warfield and the other Princeton theologians did.

off as Christian characteristics. Jesus, we are reminded, was still a man of his generation, liable to error in his human knowledge, and allowance must be made for the limitations of his conceptions and judgments. . . .[25]

Bruce K. Waltke, "Historical Grammatical Problems" (1982)

To be sure evangelicals must avoid the pitfalls of the new hermeneutics—that the recognition of the author's meaning is an impossibility, that what the text once meant can no longer be authoritative theological statement in the modern era, that the text and one's experience of it enter into a relationship of mutuality, that the interpreter and text are necessarily swallowed up in a sea of historical relativity, that the objective meaning of the text is no longer the interpreter's goal, that meaning takes place in the existential encounter between text and interpreter. Nevertheless, the practitioner of the historico-grammatical exegesis should pick up the strengths of the new hermeneutics; namely, of letting the text correct his own preunderstanding and of entering into the Bible's own culture—its facts, its "world" of ideas and values and above all its supra-historical and supra-cultural factor of conversion to the God of Israel and his Christ along with the acceptance of his Lordship over creation and history, in contrast, for example, to secularism, humanism and Marxist atheism.

By submitting in faith to these cultural dimensions of the text, conversion takes place and spiritual understanding ensues. The hermeneut is now spiritually prepared to translate the text in addition to being cognitively prepared for its historico-grammatical translation. This spiritual transformation, brought about by an encounter with the text and a decision on the part of the interpreter to surrender fully to its claims, also removes emotional blockages, political allegiances, socio-economic and other conscious or unconscious prejudices.

To be sure the so-called new hermeneutic is not altogether new.

---

[25]James Orr, "Holy Scripture and Modern Negations," in *The Fundamentals*, 4 vols., ed. R. A. Torrey et al. (1917; repr. Grand Rapids, MI: Baker, 2003), 1:96–99.

Jesus accused his critics of erring in their interpretation of Scripture for spiritual reasons (Matt. 22:29). Lady Wisdom rebuked the fools of her day: "If you had responded to my rebuke, I would have poured out my heart to you and made my thoughts known to you" (Prov. 1:23). Paul likewise emphasized spiritual understanding (1 Cor. 2:10–3:4). Although the principle of commitment to that which is being looked into has always been understood by both evangelicals, especially by those within the pietistic tradition, and by philosophers who stressed associating knowing with experience, to my knowledge it has never been consciously linked as part of the historico-grammatical method of interpretation. This positive and abiding value of the new hermeneutic is in keeping with the method of the reformers, who proposed a hermeneutical circle that sought to allow Scripture to correct the church's traditions. What is new is the stress upon correcting one's unconscious prejudices regarding the Scripture's meaning.[26]

---

[26]Bruce K. Waltke, "Historical Grammatical Problems," in *Hermeneutics, Inerrancy, and the Bible*, eds. Earl D. Radmacher and Robert D. Preus (Grand Rapids, MI: Zondervan, 1984), 77–78.

GLOSSARY

Accommodation: that God adapted divine truths and the communication of them through the written Scripture in such a way that the human mind can comprehend them.

American Baptist Churches in the USA (ABC-USA): major, broadly evangelical Baptist denomination formed in 1907; faced controversy over inerrancy in the 1920s.

American Lutheran Church (ALC): large Lutheran denomination formed in 1930 from primarily German Lutheran immigrants to the United States; later merged with other Lutheran denominations to form the Evangelical Lutheran Church in America (ELCA).

Authorial intent: the meaning a particular biblical writer intended to communicate to his audience in writing.

Barth, Karl (1886–1968): influential Swiss theologian and pastor who rejected liberalism in favor of neo-orthodoxy; authored *Church Dogmatics*; rejected the use of scientific or natural theology and defended the view that faith is necessary to understand and use Christian theology.

Berkouwer, Gerrit Cornelis (G. C.) (1903–1996): Dutch Reformed theologian who advocated the primacy of Scripture as the norm for all Christian thinking and living; authored *Studies in Dogmatics* (1952–1976); critical of Barth's theology in his early days but later favored Barth and became critical of Warfield and his followers.

Biblical criticism: encompasses the various means of critical study of the Bible (historical criticism, form criticism, etc.); another name for higher criticism.

Boice, James Montgomery (1938–2000): pastor of Tenth Presbyterian Church (PCA) in Philadelphia (1968–2000); chairman of the International Council on Biblical Inerrancy (ICBI) from its founding in 1977 to its completion in 1988; founder of the Alliance of Confessing Evangelicals (1994).

Briggs, Charles Augustus (C. A.) (1841–1913): American biblical scholar; professor at Union Theological Seminary in New York (1874–1913);

coeditor (with A. A. Hodge) of *The Presbyterian Review*; Presbyterian minister suspended in 1893 for his support of higher criticism.

Bultmann, Rudolf (1884–1976): influential German liberal theologian and New Testament scholar; skepticism over the historical accuracy of the New Testament led Bultmann to advocate discerning the supposed myths from the historical facts in the text ("demythologizing").

Canonical approach: method of theological interpretation developed in large part by Brevard S. Childs (1923–2007), professor of Old Testament at Yale University; insists that any legitimate interpretation of the Bible must accept the whole Christian canon and study it accordingly.

Chicago Statement on Biblical Hermeneutics: second statement composed by the members of the International Council on Biblical Inerrancy (ICBI), in Chicago in 1982; aimed to clarify a conservative evangelical position on hermeneutics.

Chicago Statement on Biblical Inerrancy: first statement issued by the International Council on Biblical Inerrancy (ICBI) in Chicago in 1978; carefully defines and strongly affirms an evangelical view of inerrancy.

Christotelic: from the Greek words *Christos*, meaning "Christ," and *telos*, meaning "end" or "purpose"; a reading of the Bible that sees Christ as the ultimate purpose in and for all of Scripture.

Deconstructionism: approach to knowledge that distrusts the objectivity of the interpreter and is keenly aware of the various presuppositions, prejudgments, and types of cultural conditioning to which any interpreter is subject; the term was coined by French philosopher Jacques Derrida.

Demythologization: term referring to Rudolf Bultmann's method of interpreting the New Testament; separates the reality or truth in the text from the myths, expressed in symbolic language and ancient worldviews, in which it is imbedded.

Derrida, Jacques (1930–2004): French philosopher and literary scholar who proposed the concept of deconstructionism.

Dictation theory: holds that God directly dictated to the biblical writers the exact words they were to write when they composed the scriptural text, allowing for no freedom of the individual authors.

Docetism: from the Greek word *dokeo*, meaning "to appear"; early Christian church heresy that taught that the divine Christ only appeared to be human.

Documentary hypothesis: the proposition that the Pentateuch was the result of an editor (redactor) combining four originally independent documents represented as J-E-D-P; Julius Wellhausen developed the most influential version of this hypothesis.

Ebionitism: heresy of the early centuries of the Christian church that denied the deity of Christ.

Epistemology: the branch of philosophy concerned with the study of the nature and extent of knowledge.

Evangelical Lutheran Church in America (ELCA): largest Lutheran denomination in America; formed as the result of the merging of three Lutheran denominations in 1987.

Evangelical Theological Society (ETS): organization of conservative North American biblical scholars and theologians formed in 1949; membership in the Society requires affirming the inerrancy of Scripture and the triunity of God.

"Five Point Deliverance": doctrinal statement adopted by the Presbyterian Church (USA) for use in the licensing of ministers; expansion of the Portland Deliverance of 1892 on inspiration and inerrancy.

Form criticism: an approach to literary studies that, when applied to the Bible and especially the Gospels, involves attempting to understand and classify the oral stage of Scripture's various stories and traditions.

Fosdick, Harry Emerson (1878–1969): prominent liberal Baptist pastor who rejected the virgin birth and the inerrancy of Scripture; ministered at Park Avenue Baptist Church, later Riverside Church, from 1925–1946; authored many books.

Fuller Theological Seminary: prominent evangelical seminary founded in 1947 by Charles E. Fuller and Harold John Ockenga; became a leader in the "new evangelical" or neo-evangelical movement of the middle of the twentieth century.

Grammatical-historical interpretation: method of exegetical interpretation that focuses on the context, the original languages, the genre, and the historical and cultural background of biblical passages.

Gundry, Robert H. (1933–): a professor emeritus of New Testament and Greek at Westmont College in California; expelled from the Evangelical Theological Society (ETS) for his use of redaction criticism in his book *Matthew: A Commentary on His Literary and Theological Art* (1982).

Henry, Carl F. H. (1913–2003): one of the most influential evangelical theologians of the twentieth century; served as a professor at

Fuller Theological Seminary (1950–1968); was the first editor of *Christianity Today* (1955–1968); signed the Chicago Statement on Biblical Inerrancy (1978); authored numerous books.

Hermeneutics: from the Greek name Hermes, the messenger god; the philosophy or principles that guide interpretation.

Higher criticism: approach to the study of the Bible that assumes it is primarily a human book and consequently limited and prone to errors; calls all aspects of Scripture into question and subjects all texts to scrutiny.

Hodge, Charles (1797–1878): prominent evangelical Presbyterian theologian and professor of theology at Princeton Theological Seminary (1840–1878); coeditor of the *Biblical Repertory and Princeton Review* (1824–1871); author of *Systematic Theology* (1872–1873).

Incarnational analogy: term for the relationship between Christ's incarnation and Scripture; in Christ's incarnation the divine and infinite God took on human and finite flesh, and in a similar but not identical way, in the Bible the mind of God is put into terms written and understood by humans.

Inerrancy: represents the view that the Bible, in the original autographs and correctly understood, is truthful in all that it affirms.

Infallibility: being incapable of error; often considered synonymous with inerrancy among conservative evangelicals but distinguished from inerrancy by many non-conservatives.

International Council on Biblical Inerrancy (ICBI): organization formed in 1977 to articulate and defend a conservative evangelical doctrine of inerrancy; the Council produced three major statements on inerrancy, hermeneutics, and application; ICBI disbanded in 1988, having completed its intended work.

J-E-D-P: refers to the four independent documents (or "strands") that the documentary hypothesis considers to be the original sources used in the composition of the Pentateuch; the initials represent the names of the sources: Jahwist, Elohist, Deuteronomist, and Priestly.

Lindsell, Harold (1913–1998): staunch conservative defender of the Bible's inerrancy; vice president and professor of missions at Fuller Theological Seminary until 1964; editor of *Christianity Today* (1968–1978); author of *The Battle for the Bible* (1976).

Literary criticism: approach that focuses on the Bible as literature; analyzes the various genres, inherent artistry, and final form.

"Lower" criticism: older term synonymous with the more contemporary phrase, textual criticism.

Lutheran Church in America (LCA): largest American Lutheran denomination before the merger of three denominations in 1987, which formed the Evangelical Lutheran Church in America (ELCA).

Lutheran Church-Missouri Synod: most theologically conservative body of Lutheran churches in America; organized in 1847 under the name German Evangelical Lutheran Synod of Missouri, Ohio, and Other States, dropping *German* during World War I, and changing to its current name in 1947.

Lyotard, Jean-François (1924–1998): French philosopher and literary theorist known for his articulation and analysis of postmodernism and his skepticism regarding the existence of metanarratives.

Machen, J. Gresham (1881–1937): New Testament scholar and prominent Presbyterian defender of Christian orthodoxy in America against modernism and liberalism; professor at Princeton Theological Seminary (1914–1929); founded Westminster Theological Seminary in Philadelphia (1929) and was involved in the formation of the Presbyterian Church of America (1936), later named Orthodox Presbyterian Church (OPC).

McKim, Donald K. (1950–): Presbyterian theologian (PCUSA); coauthor (with Jack B. Rogers) of *The Authority and Interpretation: An Historical Approach* (1979), from which he is identified with the Rogers/McKim proposal on inspiration and inerrancy.

Metanarrative: from the Greek word *meta*, meaning "over" or "above"; the concept in modernity that there is a master or grand story of human reality based on the assumption of absolute universal truths that purports to have an explanation for everything; strongly criticized by philosopher Jean-François Lyotard.

Narrative theology: approach to biblical theology and interpretation that favors the narrative over the historically conditioned and systematically ordered explanations of Scripture's propositions; associated with the Yale School and, in particular, professor Hans Frei.

Neo-orthodoxy: diverse theological movement primarily in the twentieth century that emphasizes, among many other things, the wholly otherness of God in relation to humans, the peculiarity of God's word written (Scripture) and living (Christ), and the effect of sin on the rational ability of the human mind; key players include Karl Barth, G. C. Berkouwer, and, to some extent, Rudolf Bultmann.

New evangelicalism: term coined by Harold John Ockenga in 1947 and also known as neo-evangelicalism; refers to the renaissance within evangelicalism following World War II, especially on the fronts of intellectual engagement and social action.

Northern Baptist Convention: name of the American Baptist Churches in the USA (ABC-USA) denomination from 1907–1950.

Portland Deliverance: statement issued by the General Assembly of the Presbyterian Church (USA) in 1892 mandating that the denomination's ministers subscribe to a strongly conservative position on inspiration and inerrancy; this statement played a prominent role in the heresy trial of Charles A. Briggs.

Presbyterian Church in the USA (PCUSA): large mainline Presbyterian denomination organized from 1983–1987 out of two smaller denominations; the scene of much controversy during the struggles between fundamentalists and modernists in the late nineteenth and early twentieth centuries.

Princetonians: refers to the thought of Archibald Alexander, Samuel Miller, Charles Hodge, A. A. Hodge, Francis L. Patton, and B. B. Warfield, all professors at Princeton Theological Seminary.

Proposition: term in philosophy and logic for any sort of meaning-filled declarative statement (idea, sentence, doctrine, etc.).

Pseudepigrapha: from two Greek words *pseudo*, meaning "false," and *grapha*, meaning "writing"; refers to books circulating at the time of the early church that were excluded from the biblical canon.

Rationalist criticism: synonymous with higher criticism.

Reader-response theory: sees the location of meaning not in the text or the author's intent but in the reader (interpreter) and his/her experience; closely associated with deconstructionism.

Redaction criticism: analyzes the author's or editor's particular uses and arrangements of sources; often used with regard to the Pentateuch and the Synoptic Gospels.

Rogers, Jack B.: Presbyterian theologian (PCUSA) and coauthor with Donald K. McKim of *The Authority and Interpretation of the Bible: An Historical Approach* (1979), from which he is identified with the Rogers/McKim proposal on inspiration and inerrancy.

Rogers/McKim proposal: proposition put forth by Jack B. Rogers and Donald K. McKim in their book *The Authority and Interpretation of the Bible: An Historical Approach* (1979) that the Princetonians, A. A. Hodge and B. B. Warfield in particular, invented the evangelical views of verbal, plenary inspiration and inerrancy, diverting from a more flexible view of Scripture espoused by earlier orthodox Christian theologians.

Rorty, Richard (1931–2007): American philosopher who focused much of his attention on modern and postmodern epistemologies, arguing that the basis of truth is not objectivity but the groups or communities that establish truth for themselves.

Situatedness: postmodern term for the subjectivity of interpretation and meaning; all texts and all interpretive communities are situated in historical and cultural settings.

Strauss, David Friedrich (1808–1874): German theologian and higher critic who dedicated much of his work to discovering the historical person of Jesus by separating the myths of the Gospels from the historical facts of Jesus' life.

Synoptic Gospels: the first three Gospel accounts—Matthew, Mark, and Luke; these Gospels are set apart from John because of the similarity in their styles and content.

Textual criticism: approach to the interpretation of the Bible that examines the variant readings of individual passages and seeks to determine which reading best represents the original autographs; exercised by both conservative and liberal scholars.

Theological interpretation: refers to the approach to interpretation that examines how the church in different times and in separate cultures and settings has interpreted Scripture with a view to contextualizing current theological questions and crises.

Theopneustos: Greek word meaning "God-breathed"; translated as "inspired" in many English Bibles.

Verbal, plenary inspiration: view of inspiration that holds that all (plenary) of the words (verbal) of Scripture are inspired by God.

Warfield, Benjamin Breckinridge (B. B.) (1851–1921): key articulator and defender of the Princetonian view of the verbal, plenary inspiration of Scripture and, by extension, inerrancy; professor of theology at Princeton Theological Seminary (1887–1921); coauthor of the pivotal article "Inspiration," with A. A. Hodge, in 1881.

Wellhausen, Julius (1844–1918): renowned German liberal biblical scholar; influential in the development of the documentary hypothesis.

Westminster Theological Seminary: founded in 1929 by J. Gresham Machen and considered an extension of "Old Princeton"; earned a reputation for conservative biblical scholarship.

Yale School: approach to biblical interpretation that focuses on narrative theology; includes key Yale Divinity School theologians Hans Frei, George Lindbeck, and David Kelsey.

APPENDIX ONE:
DOCTRINAL STATEMENTS ON
SCRIPTURE

Alliance of Confessing Evangelicals, Cambridge Declaration (1996)

We reaffirm the inerrant Scripture to be the sole source of written divine revelation, which alone can bind the conscience. The Bible alone teaches all that is necessary for our salvation from sin and is the standard by which all Christian behavior must be measured.

Evangelical Affirmations (1989)

We affirm the complete truthfulness and the full and final authority of the Old and New Testament Scriptures as the word of God written. The appropriate response to it is humble assent and obedience.

The word of God becomes effective by the power of the Holy Spirit working in and through it. Through the Scriptures the Holy Spirit creates faith and provides a sufficient doctrinal and moral guide for the church. Just as God's self-giving love to us in the gospel provides the supreme motive for the Christian life, so the teaching of Holy Scripture informs us of what are truly acts of love.

Attempts to limit the truthfulness of inspired Scripture to "faith and practice," viewed as less than the whole of Scripture, or worse, to assert that it errs in such matters as history or the world of nature, depart not only from the Bible's representation of its own veracity, but also from the central tradition of the Christian churches.

The meaning of Scripture must neither be divorced from its words nor dictated by reader response.

The inspired author's intention is essential to our understanding of the text. No Scripture must be interpreted in isolation from other passages of Scripture.

All Scripture is true and profitable, but Scripture must be interpreted by Scripture. The truth of any single passage must be understood in light of the truth of all passages of Scripture. Our Lord has been pleased to give us the whole corpus of Scripture to instruct and guide his church.[1]

---

[1] Kenneth S. Kantzer and Carl F. H. Henry, eds., *Evangelical Affirmations* (Grand Rapids, MI: Zondervan, 1990), 32–33.

Evangelical Alliance, Basis of Faith (1846)

That the parties composing the Alliance shall be such persons only as hold and maintain what are usually understood to be evangelical views, in regard to the matters of doctrine understated, namely: 1. The divine inspiration, authority, and sufficiency of the Holy Scriptures. 2. The right and duty of private judgment in the interpretation of the Holy Scriptures.

Evangelical Alliance, Basis of Faith (1970)

Evangelical Christians accept the revelation of the triune God given in the Scriptures of the Old and New Testaments and confess the historic faith of the Gospels therein set forth. They here assert the doctrines which they regard as crucial to the understanding of the faith, and which should issue in mutual love, practical Christian service and evangelistic concern. . . . The divine inspiration of the Holy Scripture and its consequent entire trustworthiness and supreme authority in all matters of faith and conduct.

Evangelical Theological Society, Doctrinal Basis (1949)

The Bible alone, and the Bible in its entirety, is the word of God written and is therefore inerrant in the autographs.

Fuller Theological Seminary, Statement of Faith (1949)

[The original Scriptures] are plenarily inspired and free from error in the whole and in the part.

Fuller Theological Seminary, Statement of Faith (1962)

Scripture is an essential part and trustworthy record of this divine self-disclosure. All the books of the Old and New Testaments, given by divine inspiration, are the written word of God, the only infallible rule of faith and practice. They are to be interpreted according to their context and purpose and in reverent obedience to the Lord who speaks through them in living power.

International Congress on World Evangelization, Lausanne Covenant (1974)

We affirm the divine inspiration and truthfulness and authority of both Old and New Testament Scriptures in their entirety as the only written word of God without error in all that it affirms and the only infallible rule of faith and practice. We also affirm the power of God's word to accomplish his purpose of salvation. The message of the Bible is addressed to all mankind. For God's revelation in Christ and in Scripture is unchangeable. Through it the Holy Spirit still speaks today. He illumines the mind of God's people in every culture to perceive its truth freshly through our own eyes and thus discloses to the whole church ever more of the many-colored wisdom of God.

International Council on Biblical Inerrancy, the Chicago Statement on Biblical Inerrancy (1978)

Preface

The authority of Scripture is a key issue for the Christian church in this and every age. Those who profess faith in Jesus Christ as Lord and Savior are called to show the reality of their discipleship by humbly and faithfully obeying God's written word. To stray from Scripture in faith or conduct is disloyalty to our Master. Recognition of the total truth and trustworthiness of Holy Scripture is essential to a full grasp and adequate confession of its authority.

The following statement affirms this inerrancy of Scripture afresh, making clear our understanding of it and warning against its denial. We are persuaded that to deny it is to set aside the witness of Jesus Christ and of the Holy Spirit and to refuse that submission to the claims of God's own word which marks true Christian faith. We see it as our timely duty to make this affirmation in the face of current lapses from the truth of inerrancy among our fellow Christians and misunderstanding of this doctrine in the world at large.

This statement consists of three parts: a summary statement, articles of affirmation and denial, and an exposition.[2] It has been prepared in the course of a three-day consultation in Chicago. Those who have signed the Summary Statement and the Articles wish to affirm their own conviction as to the inerrancy of Scripture and to encourage and challenge one another and all Christians to growing appreciation and understanding of this doctrine. We acknowledge the limitations of a document prepared in a brief, intensive conference and do not propose that this statement be given creedal weight. Yet we rejoice in the deepening of our own convictions through our discussions together, and we pray that the statement we have signed may be used to the glory of our God toward a new reformation of the Church in its faith, life, and mission.

We offer this statement in a spirit, not of contention, but of humility and love, which we purpose by God's grace to maintain in any future dialogue arising out of what we have said. We gladly acknowledge that many who deny the inerrancy of Scripture do not display the consequences of this denial in the rest of their belief and behavior, and we are conscious that we who confess this doctrine often deny it in life by failing to bring our thoughts and deeds, our traditions and habits, into true subjection to the divine word.

We invite response to this statement from any who see reason to amend its affirmations about Scripture by the light of Scripture itself, under whose infallible authority we stand as we speak. We claim no personal infallibility for the witness we bear, and for any help which enables us to strengthen this testimony to God's word we shall be grateful.

---

[2]The exposition does not appear in this reprinting of the statement.

A Short Statement

1. God, who is himself Truth and speaks truth only, has inspired Holy Scripture in order thereby to reveal himself to lost mankind through Jesus Christ as Creator and Lord, Redeemer and Judge. Holy Scripture is God's witness to himself.

2. Holy Scripture, being God's own word, written by men prepared and superintended by his Spirit, is of infallible divine authority in all matters upon which it touches: it is to be believed, as God's instruction, in all that it affirms; obeyed, as God's command, in all that it requires; embraced, as God's pledge, in all that it promises.

3. The Holy Spirit, Scripture's divine Author, both authenticates it to us by his inward witness and opens our minds to understand its meaning.

4. Being wholly and verbally God-given, Scripture is without error or fault in all its teaching, no less in what it states about God's acts in creation, about the events of world history, and about its own literary origins under God, than in its witness to God's saving grace in individual lives.

5. The authority of Scripture is inescapably impaired if this total divine inerrancy is in any way limited or disregarded, or made relative to a view of truth contrary to the Bible's own; and such lapses bring serious loss to both the individual and the church.

Articles of Affirmation and Denial

Article I

We affirm that the Holy Scriptures are to be received as the authoritative word of God.

We deny that the Scriptures receive their authority from the church, tradition, or any other human source.

Article II

We affirm that the Scriptures are the supreme written norm by which God binds the conscience, and that the authority of the church is subordinate to that of Scripture.

We deny that church creeds, councils, or declarations have authority greater than or equal to the authority of the Bible.

Article III

We affirm that the written word in its entirety is revelation given by God.

We deny that the Bible is merely a witness to revelation, or only becomes revelation in encounter, or depends on the responses of men for its validity.

Article IV

We affirm that God who made mankind in his image has used language as a means of revelation.

We deny that human language is so limited by our creatureliness that it is rendered inadequate as a vehicle for divine revelation. We further deny that the corruption of human culture and language through sin has thwarted God's work of inspiration.

Article V

We affirm that God's revelation in the Holy Scriptures was progressive.

We deny that later revelation, which may fulfill earlier revelation, ever corrects or contradicts it. We further deny that any normative revelation has been given since the completion of the New Testament writings.

Article VI

We affirm that the whole of Scripture and all its parts, down to the very words of the original, were given by divine inspiration.

We deny that the inspiration of Scripture can rightly be affirmed of the whole without the parts, or of some parts but not the whole.

Article VII

We affirm that inspiration was the work in which God by his Spirit, through human writers, gave us his word. The origin of Scripture is divine. The mode of divine inspiration remains largely a mystery to us.

We deny that inspiration can be reduced to human insight, or to heightened states of consciousness of any kind.

Article VIII

We affirm that God in his work of inspiration utilized the distinctive personalities and literary styles of the writers whom he had chosen and prepared.

We deny that God, in causing these writers to use the very words that he chose, overrode their personalities.

Article IX

We affirm that inspiration, though not conferring omniscience, guaranteed true and trustworthy utterance on all matters of which the biblical authors were moved to speak and write.

We deny that the finitude or fallenness of these writers, by necessity or otherwise, introduced distortion or falsehood into God's word.

Article X

We affirm that inspiration, strictly speaking, applies only to the autographic text of Scripture, which in the providence of God can be ascertained from available manuscripts with great accuracy. We further affirm that copies and translations of Scripture are the word of God to the extent that they faithfully represent the original.

We deny that any essential element of the Christian faith is affected by the absence of the autographs. We further deny that this absence renders the assertion of biblical inerrancy invalid or irrelevant.

Article XI

We affirm that Scripture, having been given by divine inspiration, is infallible, so that, far from misleading us, it is true and reliable in all the matters it addresses.

We deny that it is possible for the Bible to be at the same time infallible and errant in its assertions. Infallibility and inerrancy may be distinguished, but not separated.

Article XII

We affirm that Scripture in its entirety is inerrant, being free from all falsehood, fraud, or deceit.

We deny that biblical infallibility and inerrancy are limited to spiritual, religious, or redemptive themes, exclusive of assertions in the fields of history and science. We further deny that scientific hypotheses about earth history may properly be used to overturn the teaching of Scripture on creation and the flood.

Article XIII

We affirm the propriety of using inerrancy as a theological term with reference to the complete truthfulness of Scripture.

We deny that it is proper to evaluate Scripture according to standards of truth and error that are alien to its usage or purpose. We further deny that inerrancy is negated by biblical phenomena such as a lack of modern technical precision, irregularities of grammar or spelling, observational descriptions of nature, the reporting of falsehoods, the use of hyperbole and round numbers, the topical arrangement of material, variant selections of material in parallel accounts, or the use of free citations.

Article XIV

We affirm the unity and internal consistency of Scripture.

We deny that alleged errors and discrepancies that have not yet been resolved vitiate the truth claims of the Bible.

Article XV

We affirm that the doctrine of inerrancy is grounded in the teaching of the Bible about inspiration.

We deny that Jesus's teaching about Scripture may be dismissed by appeals to accommodation or to any natural limitation of his humanity.

Article XVI

We affirm that the doctrine of inerrancy has been integral to the Church's faith throughout its history.

We deny that inerrancy is a doctrine invented by scholastic Protestantism, or is a reactionary position postulated in response to negative higher criticism.

Article XVII

We affirm that the Holy Spirit bears witness to the Scriptures, assuring believers of the truthfulness of God's written word.

We deny that this witness of the Holy Spirit operates in isolation from or against Scripture.

Article XVIII

We affirm that the text of Scripture is to be interpreted by grammatical-historical exegesis, taking account of its literary forms and devices, and that Scripture is to interpret Scripture.

We deny the legitimacy of any treatment of the text or quest for sources lying behind it that leads to relativizing, dehistoricizing, or discounting its teaching, or rejecting its claims to authorship.

Article XIX

We affirm that a confession of the full authority, infallibility, and inerrancy of Scripture is vital to a sound understanding of the whole of the Christian faith. We further affirm that such confession should lead to increasing conformity to the image of Christ.

We deny that such confession is necessary for salvation. However, we further deny that inerrancy can be rejected without grave consequences, both to the individual and to the church.

International Council on Biblical Inerrancy, the Chicago Statement on Biblical Hermeneutics (1982)

Preface

Summit I of the International Council on Biblical Inerrancy took place in Chicago on October 26-28, 1978 for the purpose of affirming afresh the doctrine of the inerrancy of Scripture, making clear the understanding of it and warning against its denial. In the years that have passed since Summit I, God has blessed that effort in ways surpassing most anticipations. A gratifying flow of helpful literature on the doctrine of inerrancy as well as a growing commitment to its value give cause to pour forth praise to our great God.

The work of Summit I had hardly been completed when it became evident that there was yet another major task to be tackled. While we recognize that belief in the inerrancy of Scripture is basic to maintaining its authority, the values of that commitment are only as real as one's understanding of the meaning of Scripture. Thus, the need for Summit II. For two years plans were laid and papers were written on themes relating to hermeneutical principles and practices. The culmination of this effort has been a meeting in Chicago on November 10-13, 1982 at which we, the undersigned, have participated.

In similar fashion to the Chicago Statement of 1978, we herewith present these affirmations and denials as an expression of the results of our labors to clarify hermeneutical issues and principles. We do not claim completeness or systematic treatment of the entire subject, but these affirmations and denials represent a consensus of the approximately one hundred participants and observers gathered at this conference. It has been a broadening experience to engage in dialogue, and it is our prayer that God will use the product of our diligent efforts to enable us and others to more correctly handle the word of truth (2 Tim. 2:15).[3]

Article I

We affirm that the normative authority of Holy Scripture is the authority of God himself, and is attested by Jesus Christ, the Lord of the church.

We deny the legitimacy of separating the authority of Christ from the authority of Scripture, or of opposing the one to the other.

Article II

We affirm that as Christ is God and man in one person, so Scripture is, indivisibly, God's word in human language.

We deny that the humble, human form of Scripture entails errancy any more than the humanity of Christ, even in his humiliation, entails sin.

Article III

We affirm that the person and work of Jesus Christ are the central focus of the entire Bible.

We deny that any method of interpretation which rejects or obscures the Christ-centeredness of Scripture is correct.

Article IV

We affirm that the Holy Spirit who inspired Scripture acts through it today to work faith in its message.

We deny that the Holy Spirit ever teaches to anyone anything which is contrary to the teaching of Scripture.

Article V

We affirm that the Holy Spirit enables believers to appropriate and apply Scripture to their lives.

We deny that the natural man is able to discern spiritually the biblical message apart from the Holy Spirit.

Article VI

We affirm that the Bible expresses God's truth in propositional statements, and we declare that biblical truth is both objective and absolute. We further affirm that a statement is true if it represents matters as they actually are, but is an error if it misrepresents the facts.

We deny that, while Scripture is able to make us wise unto salvation, biblical truth should be defined in terms of this function. We further deny that error should be defined as that which willfully deceives.

Article VII

We affirm that the meaning expressed in each biblical text is single,

---

[3]The exposition segment of this statement does not appear in this reprinting.

definite and fixed. We deny that the recognition of this single meaning eliminates the variety of its application.

Article VIII

We affirm that the Bible contains teachings and mandates which apply to all cultural and situational contexts and other mandates which the Bible itself shows apply only to particular situations.

We deny that the distinctions between the universal and particular mandates of Scripture can be determined by cultural and situational factors. We further deny that universal mandates may ever be treated as culturally or situationally relative.

Article IX

We affirm that the term hermeneutics, which historically signified the rules of exegesis, may properly be extended to cover all that is involved in the process of perceiving what the biblical revelation means and how it bears on our lives.

We deny that the message of Scripture derives from, or is dictated by, the interpreter's understanding. Thus we deny that the "horizons" of the biblical writer and the interpreter may rightly "fuse" in such a way that what the text communicates to the interpreter is not ultimately controlled by the expressed meaning of the Scripture.

Article X

We affirm that Scripture communicates God's truth to us verbally through a wide variety of literary forms.

We deny that any of the limits of human language render Scripture inadequate to convey God's message.

Article XI

We affirm that translations of the text of Scripture can communicate knowledge of God across all temporal and cultural boundaries.

We deny that the meaning of biblical texts is so tied to the culture out of which they came that understanding of the same meaning in other cultures is impossible.

Article XII

We affirm that in the task of translating the Bible and teaching it in the context of each culture, only those functional equivalents which are faithful to the content of biblical teaching should be employed.

We deny the legitimacy of methods which either are insensitive to the demands of cross-cultural communication or distort biblical meaning in the process.

Article XIII

We affirm that awareness of the literary categories, formal and stylistic, of the various parts of Scripture is essential for proper exegesis, and hence we value genre criticism as one of the many disciplines of biblical study.

We deny that generic categories which negate historicity may rightly be imposed on biblical narratives which present themselves as factual.

Article XIV

We affirm that the biblical record of events, discourses and sayings, though presented in a variety of appropriate literary forms, corresponds to historical fact.

We deny that any event, discourse or saying reported in Scripture was invented by the biblical writers or by the traditions they incorporated.

Article XV

We affirm the necessity of interpreting the Bible according to its literal, or normal, sense. The literal sense is the grammatical-historical sense, that is, the meaning which the writer expressed. Interpretation according to the literal sense will take account of all figures of speech and literary forms found in the text.

We deny the legitimacy of any approach to Scripture that attributes to it meaning which the literal sense does not support.

Article XVI

We affirm that legitimate critical techniques should be used in determining the canonical text and its meaning.

We deny the legitimacy of allowing any method of biblical criticism to question the truth or integrity of the writer's expressed meaning, or of any other scriptural teaching.

Article XVII

We affirm the unity, harmony and consistency of Scripture and declare that it is its own best interpreter.

We deny that Scripture may be interpreted in such a way as to suggest that one passage corrects or militates against another. We deny that later writers of Scripture misinterpreted earlier passages of Scripture when quoting from or referring to them.

Article XVIII

We affirm that the Bible's own interpretation of itself is always correct, never deviating from, but rather elucidating, the single meaning of the inspired text. The single meaning of a prophet's words includes, but is not restricted to, the understanding of those words by the prophet and necessarily involves the intention of God evidenced in the fulfillment of those words.

We deny that the writers of Scripture always understood the full implications of their own words.

Article XIX

We affirm that any preunderstandings which the interpreter brings to Scripture should be in harmony with scriptural teaching and subject to correction by it.

We deny that Scripture should be required to fit alien preunderstandings, inconsistent with itself, such as naturalism, evolutionism, scientism, secular humanism, and relativism.

Article XX

We affirm that since God is the author of all truth, all truths, biblical and extra-biblical, are consistent and cohere, and that the Bible speaks truth when it touches on matters pertaining to nature, history, or anything else. We further affirm that in some cases extra-biblical data have value for clarifying what Scripture teaches, and for prompting correction of faulty interpretations.

We deny that extra-biblical views ever disprove the teaching of Scripture or hold priority over it.

Article XXI

We affirm the harmony of special with general revelation and therefore of biblical teaching with the facts of nature.

We deny that any genuine scientific facts are inconsistent with the true meaning of any passage of Scripture.

Article XXII

We affirm that Genesis 1-11 is factual, as is the rest of the book.

We deny that the teachings of Genesis 1-11 are mythical and that scientific hypotheses about earth history or the origin of humanity may be invoked to overthrow what Scripture teaches about creation.

Article XXIII

We affirm the clarity of Scripture and specifically of its message about salvation from sin.

We deny that all passages of Scripture are equally clear or have equal bearing on the message of redemption.

Article XXIV

We affirm that a person is not dependent for understanding of Scripture on the expertise of biblical scholars.

We deny that a person should ignore the fruits of the technical study of Scripture by biblical scholars.

Article XXV

We affirm that the only type of preaching which sufficiently conveys the divine revelation and its proper application to life is that which faithfully expounds the text of Scripture as the word of God.

We deny that the preacher has any message from God apart from the text of Scripture.

International Fellowship of Evangelical Students, Doctrinal Basis (1947)

The divine inspiration and entire trustworthiness of Holy Scripture, as originally given, and its supreme authority in all matters of faith and conduct.

InterVarsity Christian Fellowship/USA, Doctrinal Basis (2000)

We believe in . . . the unique divine inspiration, entire trustworthiness and authority of the Bible.

The Ligonier Statement (1973)

We believe the Holy Scriptures of the Old and New Testaments to be the inspired and inerrant word of God: We hold the Bible, as originally given through human agents of revelation, to be infallible and see this as a crucial article of faith with implications for the entire life and practice of all Christian people. With the great fathers of Christian history we declare our confidence in the total trustworthiness of the Scriptures, urging that any view which imputes to them a lesser degree of inerrancy than total, is in conflict with the Bible's self-testimony in general and with the teaching of Jesus Christ in particular. Out of obedience to the Lord of the church we submit ourselves unreservedly to his authoritative view of Holy Writ.

National Association of Evangelicals, Statement of Faith (1943)

We believe the Bible to be the inspired, the only infallible, authoritative word of God.

United Presbyterian Church in the United States of America, Presbyterian Confession of 1967

The one sufficient revelation of God is Jesus Christ, the word of God incarnate, to whom the Holy Spirit bears unique and authoritative witness through the Holy Scriptures, which are received and obeyed as the word of God written. The Scriptures are not a witness among others, but the witness without parallel. The church has received the books of the Old and New Testaments as prophetic and apostolic testimony in which it hears the word of God and by which its faith and obedience are nourished and regulated.

The New Testament is the recorded testimony of apostles to the coming of the Messiah, Jesus of Nazareth, and the sending of the Holy Spirit to the church. The Old Testament bears witness to God's faithfulness in his covenant with Israel and points the way to the fulfillment of his purpose in Christ. The Old Testament is indispensable to understanding the New, and is not itself fully understood without the New.

The Bible is to be interpreted in the light of its witness to God's work of reconciliation in Christ. The Scriptures, given under the guidance of the Holy Spirit, are nevertheless the words of men, conditioned by the language, thought forms, and literary fashions of the places and times at which they were written. They reflect views of life, history, and the cosmos which were then current. The church, therefore, has an obligation to approach the Scriptures with literary and historical understanding. As God has spoken his word in diverse cultural situations, the church is confident that he will continue to speak through the Scriptures in a changing world and in every form of human culture.

God's word is spoken to his church today where the Scriptures are faithfully preached and attentively read in dependence on the illumination of the Holy Spirit and with readiness to receive their truth and direction.

Universities and Colleges Christian Fellowship, Doctrinal Basis (1947)

The Bible, as originally given, is the inspired and infallible word of God. It is the supreme authority in all matters of belief and behaviour.

World Christian Fundamentals Association, Doctrinal Statement (1919)

We believe in the Scripture of the Old and New Testaments as verbally inspired of God, and inerrant in the original writings, and that they are of supreme and final authority in faith and life.

World Congress of Fundamentalists, Congress Resolutions (1976)

A fundamentalist is a born-again believer in the Lord Jesus Christ who maintains an immovable allegiance to the inerrant, infallible, and verbally inspired Bible.

World Evangelical Alliance, Statement of Faith (1951)

We believe in the Holy Scriptures as originally given by God, divinely inspired, infallible, entirely trustworthy; and the supreme authority in all matters of faith and conduct.

APPENDIX TWO:
KEY BIBLICAL TEXTS ON THE
DOCTRINE OF SCRIPTURE

Numbers 23:19
Deuteronomy 6:6–7
Deuteronomy 8:3
2 Samuel 7:28
Psalm 1:1–2
Psalm 12:6
Psalm 119
Proverbs 30:5
Matthew 4:4
Matthew 5:18
Matthew 24:35
John 10:35
John 17:17
Acts 24:14
Romans 15:4
2 Timothy 3:14–16
Hebrews 1:1–2
James 1:22–27
1 Peter 1:22–25
2 Peter 1:16–21
2 Peter 3:15–18

APPENDIX THREE:
A GUIDE FOR FURTHER READING

SELECT BOOKS ON INSPIRATION

Donald G. Bloesch. *Holy Scripture: Revelation, Inspiration, and Interpretation* (Downers Grove, IL: InterVarsity, 1994).

A. A. Hodge and B. B. Warfield. "Inspiration," *The Presbyterian Review* 2 (April 1881): 225–260.

I. Howard Marshall. *Biblical Inspiration* (London: Hodder and Stoughton, 1982).

J. I. Packer. *"Fundamentalism" and the Word of God* (Grand Rapids, MI: Eerdmans, 1958).

B. B. Warfield. "The Biblical Idea of Inspiration," in *The Inspiration and Authority of the Bible*, ed. Samuel G. Craig (Phillipsburg, NJ: P&R, 1948).

SELECT BOOKS ON INERRANCY

G. K. Beale. *The Erosion of Inerrancy in Evangelicalism: Responding to New Challenges to Biblical Authority* (Wheaton, IL: Crossway Books, 2008).

Norman L. Geisler, ed. *Inerrancy* (Grand Rapids, MI: Zondervan, 1980).

John D. Hannah, ed. *Inerrancy and the Church* (Chicago: Moody Press, 1984).

Harold Lindsell. *The Battle for the Bible* (Grand Rapids, MI: Zondervan, 1976).

Westminster Seminary faculty. *The Infallible Word* (Phillipsburg, NJ: P&R, 1967).

Edward J. Young. *Thy Word Is Truth* (Grand Rapids, MI: Eerdmans, 1957).

SELECT BOOKS ON INTERPRETATION

David Alan Black and David S. Dockery, eds. *New Testament Criticism and Interpretation* (Grand Rapids, MI: Zondervan, 1991).

D. A. Carson and John D. Woodbridge, eds. *Hermeneutics, Authority, and Canon* (Grand Rapids, MI: Zondervan, 1986).

Vern S. Poythress. *God-Centered Biblical Interpretation* (Phillipsburg, NJ: P&R, 1999).

Earl D. Radmacher and Robert D. Preus, eds. *Hermeneutics, Inerrancy, and the Bible* (Grand Rapids, MI: Zondervan, 1984).

Moisés Silva, ed. *Foundations of Contemporary Interpretation* (Grand Rapids, MI: Zondervan, 1996).